The Complete Yurt Handbook

Paul King

eco-logic books

For Catherine

First published in 2001 by eco-logic books
Reprinted 2004
Reprinted 2007

ISBN (10) 1 899233 08 3
ISBN (13) 978 1 899233 08 3

Illustrations & Photography: Paul King
Design & Typesetting: Steven Palmer
Cover Design: Duncan Weir
Printing & Binding: Russell Press

Further copies of this book can be purchased from:
eco-logic books, Mulberry House, Maple Grove, Bath, BA2 3AF
www.eco-logicbooks.com

eco-logic books publishes, promotes and sells by mail order books that promote practical solutions to environmental problems, sustainable development, permaculture, organic gardening, green building and related topics.

Disclaimer - whilst every effort has been made to ensure the accuracy of the plans, systems and methods described, the publisher and author take no responsibility for their implementation and outcome.

acknowledgements

I would like to thank the following people who's help has made this work possible. **Jargal** the Gobi ger-maker, and **Khart Dorj**, the Ulaan Bataar ger Maker. **Munkhtuya Lundeg** and **Cristo Gavilla Gomez**, of the Mongolian Artisan's Aid Foundation, who introduced me to yurt makers and helped to fill many of the gaps in my research. **Batkhishig Palam** and **Gana Genden**, who introduced me to numerous Mongol yurt dwellers. **Mark Glen** and **Altanzul Yondonjalbuu**, who provided the authentic Mongolian recipes. Above all, thanks to my wife **Catherine** for her support and encouragement both with the book and with woodland yurts, without which I would have been forced to go and get a 'proper job' years ago.

contents

contents

PART TWO: YURT CONSTRUCTION

contents

PRONUNCIATION OF MONGOLIAN WORDS

The names of yurt components, written in italic are English transliterations of the Mongolian words. The pronunciation of a word may therefore differ somewhat from the spelling. For example the word *khana* is pronounced haan, and *Bagana* sounds more like baghan. The addition of 'h' after a letter gives it a more throaty sound, for example 'kh' has the sound of the 'ch' in the Scottish loch.

MONGOLIAN	ENGLISH	PRONUNCIATION
Ger	Mongolian yurt	Gair
Khana	Wall section	Haan
Bagana	Upright post	Baghan
Uni	Roof pole	Oon
Khalka	Kalka Mongol	Halh
Tono	Yurt crown	Tonn
Chagata	Crown securing rope	Chaght
Arak	Mare's milk vodka	Arkh

When I made my first yurt back in 1991, few people had heard of, let alone seen one. At best 'yurt' was known as a high scoring word in Scrabble. During the ten years since then the yurt has found its way into the English vocabulary. Nowadays I am rarely asked: "What is a yurt?" It has almost replaced the tipi as an alternative dwelling, whilst finding many and varied uses in mainstream society. Despite its increasing popularity, detailed information on the yurt, in particular the Mongolian ger, is almost impossible to find. Most of the information in this book is the result of direct observations and measurement taken in Mongolia.

Part One of this book will describe the various types of yurt and focus on the Mongolian ger, the type in most common use today. Part Two will give all the information necessary to build a yurt of your own.

For many centuries, throughout Central Asia, home, to most of the population has consisted of a collapsible circular framework of wooden poles, covered with felt. This robust, yet portable dwelling is commonly known as the yurt. The yurt is essentially a portable dwelling, a task to which it is perfectly suited. However, when in place it has the character of a permanent building. There is no fear of the yurt being blown down, or of the harsh weather outside intruding into the warm and orderly interior. There are no guy-ropes to adjust or flapping canvas.

In modern Mongolia the tendency towards urbanisation has not led people to abandon their yurts. People have simply brought their yurts to the city and set them up in extensive suburbs. The ger suburbs of Ulaan Baatar contain some 50,000 yurts, which house nearly half of the population. Here the yurt becomes a desirable town house with its own enclosed garden and outbuildings, the buildings being for storage or as a kennel for the dog. During the cold winters people dwelling in the dreary concrete apartment blocks, with unreliable and inadequate heating, envy their neighbours who sit around a hot stove in their yurt insulated with up to six thick layers of felt.

The proven virtues of the yurt as a portable dwelling are gradually being realised in the West, with new yurt manufacturers appearing in England and America. Yurts are being used as homes, offices, workshops, meditation spaces, spare rooms, banqueting halls, places of worship, saunas, summerhouses and for wedding receptions.

The word yurt is an anglicised version of the Russian word Yurta, which, in turn, is derived from the Turcic yurt describing a campsite, and not a trellis-framed tent. Similarly the word ger is actually the Mongolian word for home; however these terms are generally understood by English-speaking people as describing the tent itself. So for the purposes of this book, the word Yurt refers to the circular trellis-framed tents which are its subject and the word Ger describes the Mongolian yurt.

PART ONE

THE YURT

CHAPTER 1

When, where and why?

HISTORY

Their huts or tents are formed of rods covered with felt, and being exactly round, and nicely put together, they can gather them into one bundle and make them up as packages, which they carry along with them in their migrations, upon a sort of car with four wheels.

Marco Polo, (1254-1329). The Travels.
Translated by W. Marsden (1818).

Nomadic peoples leave few written or archaeological records of their passing. So early evidence of the history of the yurt is hard to find. Descriptions from ancient travellers and some frozen remains offer hints, but no absolute proof of yurt use. Herodotus (c480-c425 BC) described *ger*-carts and felt tents being used by the Scythian people. A cart found in a 2500-year-old Pazaryck grave in Southern Siberia demonstrate that all of the technologies needed to build a yurt were available at that time. But firm evidence from before the time of Ghengis Khan is hard to find.

The evolution of the modern *ger* almost certainly began in prehistoric times with a tipi-like structure, still used by the reindeer breeders of Northern Mongolia and Siberia.

The addition of a simple wall of crossed poles was the next step. This design was further refined with the addition of collapsible *khana* and bentwood poles (*fig 1*).

The early Mongolian *ger* had a curved, bottle shaped profile, and was often permanently mounted on a cart, pulled by oxen. *Ger* carts were in common use during the reign of Genghis Khan (1162-1227 AD). The entire Mongol Empire was administered from a large *ger*-cart. Modern collapsible *gers* were also in common use at this time.

In 1245-1247 Pope Innocent IV sent Friar Giovanni DiPlano Carpini, on a mission to offer Christianity to the Mongols whilst also finding out as much as possible about their origins and habits. At this time all of Europe was in fear of another Mongol invasion. Carpini travelled for two and a half years, reaching, though not actually visiting, the ancient Mongol capital of Kharakorum, and being present at the enthronement of Guyuk Khan, he described the Mongol dwellings thus:

Tartar homes are round and prepared like tents made cleverly of laths and sticks. In the middle of the roof there is a round window through which light

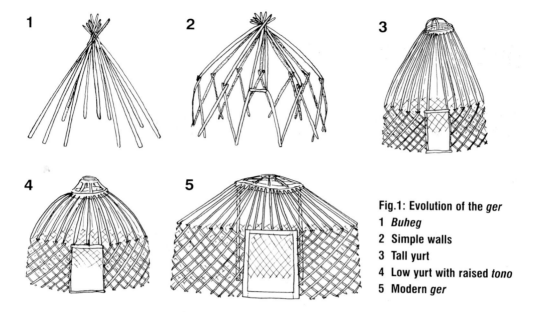

Fig.1: Evolution of the *ger*
1 *Buheg*
2 Simple walls
3 Tall yurt
4 Low yurt with raised *tono*
5 Modern *ger*

comes in and smoke can leave, because they always have a fire in the centre. The walls and the roof are covered by felt and even the doors are made of felt. Some huts are large and some are small, depending upon the wealth or poverty of the owners. Some are taken apart quickly and put back together again and carried everywhere; some cannot be taken apart and are moved on carts. The smallest are put on a cart drawn by one ox, the larger by two or three or more depending upon how large it is and how many are needed to move it. Whenever they travel, whether to war or other places, they always take their homes with them.

Friar Giovanni DiPlano Carpini, The story of the Mongols whom we call the Tartars. Trans: Erik Hildinger, 1996

The earliest complete yurt yet discovered was found in a 12th century grave in the Khentai Mountains of Northern Mongolia. This yurt was almost identical to *gers* used in the area today. Genghis Khan's armies were housed in collapsible yurts very similar to the modern *ger*, while the Khan himself lived and held court in one of many *gers* permanently mounted on carts pulled by oxen. These wheeled *gers* or *gerlugs* were typically 30 feet (9m) in diameter and pulled by 22 bulls. The shape of these *gerlugs* was rounded in profile with a raised top (*fig 2*).

The major change in *ger* design in the eight centuries since the time of Genghis Khan is the shape of the *tono*

Fig. 2: Genghis Khan's *ger* cart pulled by oxen (13th century)

which is now lower, giving a smoother roof profile.

Geography

Mongolia is the great stronghold of the yurt, where the *ger* is still home to three-quarters of the population. To the south, the inner Mongolia region of China is populated by *ger*-dwellers. To the north, the people of Tuva and the Buryat region of Siberia live in *gers*. In Eastern Siberia, the reindeer-herding Koryak people live in yurt-like *yarangas*.

The southernmost range of the bentwood yurt, where it is still in common use by nomadic peoples, covers Iran, Iraq, Northern Afghanistan and Pakistan. To the west of Mongolia, in Kazakstan, Kirgistan, Uzbekistan, Tajikistan and North-Eastern China, a region as a whole formerly known as Turkestan, the yurt is the traditional and still popular nomadic dwelling. The national flag of the newly independent Kirgistan depicts a red yurt-crown at its centre. During the middle ages the Magyars of Hungary dwelt in yurts, where they are still in occasional use today. Bentwood yurts were used in Central and Eastern Turkey until the 1960s (*fig 3*).

The virtues of yurts

As well as being an attractive and novel tent the yurt is probably the most practical temporary dwelling available, being:

● **Portable**, a yurt with a twelve foot (3.7m) (or larger) diameter can be easily carried in a small car, on a horse, in a handcart or even on a train or bus.

● **Secure**, the yurt can be fitted with a wooden door, which can be locked. The lattice-work walls ensure that entry cannot be gained even if the canvas is cut.

● **Stable**, once the yurt has been set up it has the feel of a solid building, rather than a tent; there is no flapping canvas, constant adjustment of guy ropes, or fear of leaks.

● **Weatherproof,** the fact that it has proven

Fig. 3: Yurt distribution

itself in the cold, wind, rain and snow of Mongolia for 25 centuries is evidence for this.

● **Warm in winter**, being circular with a relatively low roof it is easy and efficient to heat. The yurt was traditionally heated by an open fire, but a metal stove is more commonly used today. Insulating layers can be sandwiched between the frame and cover. Felt is the traditional insulating material but blankets, carpets, or underlay can be used.

● **Cool in summer**, the sides of the yurt can be rolled up or removed to admit a cooling breeze; for privacy the canvas or felt walls can be replaced with reed mats.

● **Inconspicuous**, despite having ample headroom, the overall height of the structure is only about seven feet (two metres) allowing it to be hidden from unwanted attention by a hedge or scrub.

● **Easy to erect**, with a little practice the yurt can be erected or taken down in less than half an hour. It is not difficult for one person to erect.

● **Easy to move**, if you decide that you have pitched your *ger* in the wrong place you can, with the help of a few friends, pick up the entire yurt and move it without any need to take it down and re-erect it.

● **Inexpensive**, it is easy to spend over £500 on the materials alone to build a yurt. But, with a bit of imagination, shopping around, and luck, it is quite easy to build one for well under £100, (or even for nothing at all, if you are lucky).

● **Easy to build**, anyone with a very basic knowledge of woodwork, sewing, a few simple tools and plenty of spare time can build a yurt. Part Two of this book will show you how.

● **Environmentally friendly**, coppicing of hazel, ash, chestnut or oak to provide poles prolongs the life of the tree and enhances the fauna and flora of the woodland. The yurt is a low-impact dwelling, causing no permanent damage to the land on which it is pitched. It can even be moved every few days to prevent the grass underneath being killed.

● **Long lasting**, with a water and rot-proof cover the yurt can stand outside for several years without harm. If only used occasionally it should last indefinitely. Broken components are easy to replace. Mongolian families near Ulaan Baatar expect a yurt frame to last up to 100 years. A 30 year-old frame looks none the worse for wear. Felts last 10–20 years and canvas should survive 10–15 years of constant use.

● **Fun!** Wherever you stay in your *ger* it is sure to attract the interest of fellow campers, it is so much more than just another boring tent. For children and adults alike yurt camping is a real break from the usual holiday accommodation. Impress your friends by swinging from the crown! The sight of a complete yurt being carried from the inside, apparently a walking tent, always raises a laugh.

CHAPTER 2

Structure

Spreading our five trellis walls like folded brocade,
Interlocking their criss-cross patterns, a conversation en
tête-à-tête,
Let us set up the trellis walls, a circle in the blue plain,
Each lath on the five petals of a cherished early flower,
Steeped in the blessed scent of thyme.

The morning star smiles above the lintel:
Let us set up our door-posts, saluting the noon day
sun,
Framing the far outlines of cloud and mountain,
Watching over our countless herds
Leading true friends to us and honoured guests.

Above the three cross-bars which confirm our faith
The blue depth of the eternal sky opens our hearts,
Let us raise up the high roof ring at the true centre
Which does not weaken the sun's radiance in the face
of the day,
Which does not dull the moonlight in the chill of
evening.

Called from every corner of the earth to meet at this
one spot,
Let us, each one, raise up the roof pole's many spokes
In homage to the precious emblem of our nation,

Symbol of the highest good which cannot be tarnished
Of faith in a unity which cannot be taken from us.

Let us set round the felt walls like the sacred frontiers
of the land which bore us,
Gage and affirmation of eternal tranquility and joy,
Whispering 'may ill not seep through', on the south
side,
Let us spread the lamb-white roof-felt, wide as the
firmament,
Whispering 'may the whirlwind not scatter us', on the
north side,
Let us lap the felt cover which knows the storms of
our three seasons, past, present and to come,
Let us make the ropes all fast, strong as the marriage
alliance.

Bringing together our fellows from near and far
In our Mongol land, cradle of our days,
In the image of our globe as it spun into being,
Rivalling the countless lofty places of the world,
Let us, all for all, raise up the great white tent.

The White Felt Tent, by Sendenjavyn Dulam
(in Dojoogyn Tsedev, 1989)

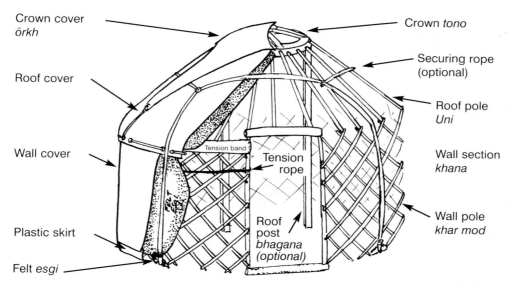

Crown cover
örkh

Crown *tono*

Securing rope
(optional)

Roof cover

Roof pole
Uni

Wall cover

Tension band

Tension
rope

Wall section
khana

Plastic skirt

Roof
post
bhagana
(optional)

Wall pole
khar mod

Felt *esgi*

Fig. 4: Dissected yurt showing major components

How the yurt works

The yurt is a self-supporting structure; the frame holds its shape with no help from guy ropes or a stretched cover. In all but the strongest winds the yurt will stand with nothing but gravity attaching it to the ground. This rigidity is maintained by opposing forces exerted by different parts of the frame. The walls are firmly tied to the door frame to form a complete, but, on it its own, fragile circle. The conical or domed roof, with its heavy crown exerts a force on top of the walls, which if left unchecked would force the sides outwards. This outward force is kept in check and put to advantage by one or more strong bands tied tightly around top of the wall. These opposing

forces give the frame great rigidity, which increases with the addition of downward pressure from a heavy roof cover and the inward pressure from tight wall covers (*fig 5*).

The yurt has an aerodynamic shape, the wind slips over the structure with a minimum of resistance. The only problem with wind can occur if a strong gust enters through the door, which can lift the yurt. For this reason the Mongolian *ger* is always pitched facing south; away from the prevailing North wind. In an old-style *ger* with a raised crown the *tono* and the *örkh* form a *venturi*, whereby the wind helps draw smoke out. The Mongol *ger* has a fairly low roof to shed wind easily (*fig 6*). In the wetter, less windswept region of Chinese

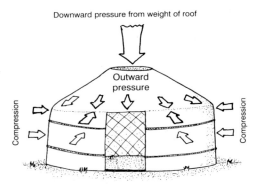

Fig. 5: Opposing pressures which give the yurt its inherent rigidity

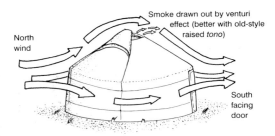

Fig. 6: Airflow over the Mongolian yurt

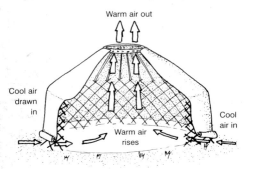

Fig. 7: Airflow inside the yurt during hot weather

Turkestan a higher roof is used to increase water run–off.

In hot weather the sides can be lifted: warm air rises and exits through the open *tono* drawing cool air in at the bottom (*fig 7*).

The frame

The yurt frame consists of four elements, all of which vary, depending on its ethnic origin. These four essential parts are, the trellis wall *khana*, the roof poles *uni*, the crown *tono*, and the door or door frame *nars* (*fig 8*).

The cover provides shelter and insulation for the yurt but, unlike that of a ridge, Tibetan, or Arab black tent is not an integral part, without which the tent will not stand. The weight of the cover does, however, add to the inherent stability of the frame. The frame is of sawn or cleft timber or round poles. The choice of timber is largely dictated by what is available locally.

The wall *khana*

The wall consists of a number of collapsible trellis panels or *khana* which are tied end-to-end to form a circle. Each panel consists of a number of poles drilled at regular intervals and fastened together. Traditionally, short knotted leather thongs are used to hold the *khana* rods together. String, metal rivets, bent nails, or nuts and bolts can also be used. Generally 16-24 full-length poles are used to produce each *khana*. The ends of each panel are made square using shorter lengths of

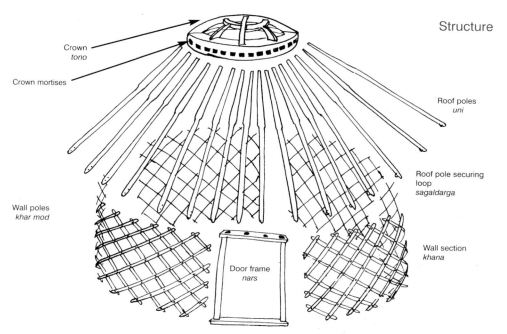

Crown
tono

Crown mortises

Roof poles
uni

Roof pole securing
loop
sagaldarga

Wall poles
khar mod

Door frame
nars

Wall section
khana

Fig. 8: Component parts of the yurt frame

drilled pole. The *khana* has a distinct top and bottom, the crossed top ends of the poles are called the heads or *tolgoi*, and the bottoms are called the feet or *ers*. A typical *khana* has 15 heads.

A number of *khana*, usually between three and six, are tied end to end to form the wall. The ends of two connecting *khana* interlock and are lashed together using horsehair rope or tapes. The two free ends either fit into a recess in the door frame, or are tied to the frame posts.

Khana poles *khar mod*
The wall rods are either of sawn or cleft slats, rectangular in section, generally 1½ x ½ inches (38x13mm), or of roundwood poles

***Ger* frame under construction in Ulaan Baatar (Mongolia)**

◀

A Mongol *ger* in the Gobi Desert showing the concave wall profile resulting from the use of straight wall poles

about one inch (25mm) in diameter. In Mongolia the rods are always between six and seven feet (1.8-2.1m) long, giving a wall height of five feet (1.5m). These poles can be shorter resulting in a lower wall height, eg. 60 inch (1.5m) poles give a four foot (1.2m) wall and 54 inch (1.37m) poles will give a 42 inch (1.07m) high wall.

The walls of most Mongolian, and all Khazak and Turkic yurts are parallel, slightly convex, or conical in profile. This shape is achieved by applying a permanent bend to each wall pole. To give a convex profile, with the yurt diameter at the top being equal to that at the bottom, a single curve along the entire length of the pole is used. The Mongol *ger* has a slightly conical profile with the diameter at

the top of the wall being slightly smaller than that at the bottom. This shape is most easily achieved by applying a single curve to the top third of the pole. More elaborate double or triple curves can give a better profile (*fig 9*).

The *khana* poles need not be bent. Straight poles are easy to manufacture, and give the standing wall of the *ger* a slightly concave profile. More care is needed to form the wall into a perfect circle when erecting the yurt. The concave shape becomes more pronounced in smaller yurts, but even in the smallest yurts this does not adversely affect the performance. Modern American, some English and many traditional Mongolian yurts have straight wall poles (*fig 10*).

Hole spacing

The spacing of the holes and the consequent rod crossover distance has a great effect on the overall strength, weight, cost, and construction time of the yurt.

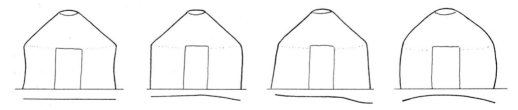

Fig. 9: Wall pole shapes (bottom), which give distinctive profiles to the assembled yurt (above)

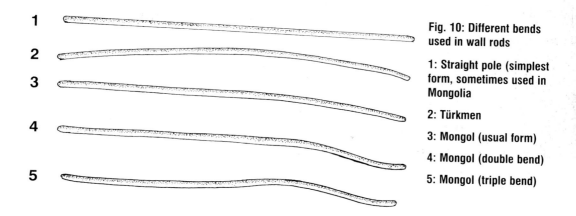

Fig. 10: Different bends used in wall rods

1: Straight pole (simplest form, sometimes used in Mongolia

2: Türkmen

3: Mongol (usual form)

4: Mongol (double bend)

5: Mongol (triple bend)

Felt, the traditional covering of the yurt, has limited tensile strength, and must therefore be supported by a close underlying framework. Therefore the spacing of wall and roof poles on a traditional yurt is closer than is necessary on a modern yurt with a strong canvas cover. Mongolian yurts have hole/crossover spacings of 6-7 inches (15-18cm). English-made yurts with strong canvas covers have spacings of nine (23cm) or even twelve inches (30cm). American yurtmakers use spacings of up to 16 inches (40cm).

Wall rods with nine or more crossover points do not, traditionally, have holes and knots at two or three of these points. The position of these free crossovers is the same throughout central Asia. They allow the *khana* to form a circle more easily as the rods slide over one another slightly at these points.

The Roof poles *uni*

The roof is supported by a number of poles, which radiate from the central *tono* out to the *khana* heads. Rarely a small simple yurt dispenses with the *tono*, the top ends of the *uni* being tied together, tipi style. In its simplest form each *uni* consists of a roundwood pole with a string loop at one end. The top end is shaped, either round or square in section, usually tapered slightly to fit into one of a number of corresponding sockets in the edge of the *tono*. In all traditional Mongolian *gers*, modern American and many modern English-made yurts the *uni* are straight. On Turkmen, Khazak, Khirgiz, and Uzbek yurts, as well as many modern English yurts the bottom ends of the *uni* are steam-bent, effectively increasing the wall height above that of the *khana*.

The Crown *tono*

The styles of traditional *tono* can be divided into two distinct types. The bentwood crown, of the Turkmen, Khazak and Khirgiz yurt, and the heavy timber crown of the Mongol *ger*. Both types have major features in common, the differences in construction will be discussed later. The *tono* consists of a circular wooden wheel, traditionally between three and six feet (1-2m) in diameter. Round holes or square mortises are made in the rim, pointing up at an angle of 20-35°). The top ends of the *uni* fit into these holes. The centre of the wheel contains a number of spokes, made from sawn (or cleft) timber or thin roundwood rods. These spokes form a raised centre, which supports the waterproof *örkh* or crown cover.

Throughout the more southern yurt lands, reed matting replaces felt for the wall covering during hot weather. This admits cool winds whilst providing shelter and security. In Mongolia the bottoms of felt walls are lifted in hot weather for ventilation. In winter up to five extra layers of felt are added. Many modern Mongolian yurts are covered with a lightweight white cotton cover, which is purely decorative, being neither waterproof, nor fire retardant. More practical, but less attractive waterproof Russian canvas covers are occasionally used over the felt.

Modern English and American yurts are covered with water and fire-proof cotton canvas or PVC, and often contain clear windows.

The Cover

The traditional yurt cover material is felt, made by beating and rolling wet sheep fleece. The wool has excellent insulation properties and its natural oils give a degree of water resistance. The felt cover is made in large pieces, the wall cover is usually in three parts. The roof consists of two or more overlapping sections.

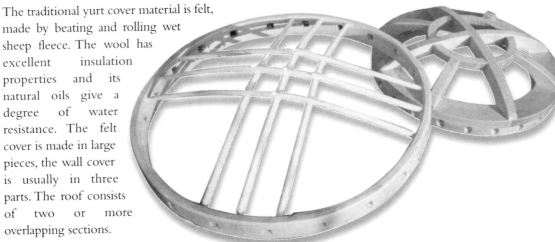

CHAPTER 3

Life in the Mongolian *ger*

In a charming field
Covered with multi-coloured flowers,
In the spacious Khanghai land
Rich in green green grass
Floats a fast river
Flooding its banks
And those thousand herds
Graze in their pleasant pasture
There stand silver-white gers
Like pearly hail
Beautifying our Mongol country
As though a shining crystal ray.

Purevyn Khorloo (in Modern Mongolian Poetry 1989)

Life, for the majority of Mongolian people, has changed little since before the time of Ghengis Khan. Despite centuries of political domination, first by the Chinese and then the Russians, the Mongols have remained true to, and fiercely proud of, their traditional ways. A portrait of the national hero, Ghengis Khan, often shares a place on the *khoimor*, with Buddhist images and family photographs.

Life in Mongolia is always hard, whether in the Taiga forests to the North, the open steppe or the Gobi desert in the South. The mainstay of the economy is Pastoral Nomadism; a family's wealth is its livestock. Arable farming is looked down upon. Less than one per cent of Mongolia's land is under cultivation.

Climate

Mongolia is a windswept land of short summers and long, cold winters. There is little precipitation: unbroken sunshine for 260 days per year gives Mongolia its title 'Land of the Blue Sky'.

The winters are as bad as anywhere in the world. Indeed, the Mongols often refer to winter as the 'killing season', due to the huge annual losses of livestock to the weather. Winter lasts from October until April: temperatures regularly drop to -30°C in Ulaan Bataar, and may fall as low as -50°C in the mountainous Western regions. Summer lasts from July until September, when the weather is pleasantly warm. Most of the annual rainfall of just 20-30cm falls during these months. Cold northerly winds of up to 60mph (96km/h) can blow in from Siberia at any time of year, particularly during the spring, producing dust storms in the desert and spreading fires through the *ger* suburbs of Ulaan Baatar.

Livestock

The Mongolians talk of the five animals: horse, cow, camel, sheep and goat; these are the livelihood and wealth of the nomadic family. The *khoimor*, or altar, of the *ger*, often displays effigies of these animals: they are so important to survival.

Numbers of livestock is measured in *Bod*, a horse, cow, or yak equals one *bod*, a camel is 1.5 *bod*. A sheep or goat equals one *bog*, seven to ten *bog* equals one *bod*. Herds are generally a mixture of all five species except in the North where there are few, or no, camels. An average family owns between 50 and 120 *bod*.

The number of animals a family has is considered a measure of its wealth. Throughout central Asia 50 animals is generally accepted as the minimum herd size to support a family. The family with a larger herd is wealthy but must work harder to maintain the animals, and grazing may be limited. Therefore there is an upper limit to herd size.

Every nomad family has at least one dog, notoriously vicious, protecting the family from

Mongol dog guarding the family *ger* and livestock

intruders and the flocks from wolves. Even Ghengis Khan used to fear the Mongols' dog. The greeting *nokhoikhor*, literally 'hold the dog', should be shouted when approaching a *ger*. The dog is never allowed inside the *ger* and is called *chirig* (soldier) or *bataar* (hero) or some equally heroic name to match its fearsome reputation.

Felt making

As well as supplying meat and dairy products and dung to fuel the stove the Mongol sheep provides the entire cover for the yurt. When wet wool is beaten and rolled it forms felt – the traditional covering material for the Mongol *ger*.

Felt is made during late summer using washed fleeces. The clean wool is spread on the ground and beaten with sticks to separate the fibres. An old felt or 'mother felt' is spread on the ground and the beaten wool is spread on top of it. Wool is added a handful at a time. Each handful is teased out to spread the fibres in one direction. Wool is added to form a uniform layer about an inch (25mm) thick. A second layer is added with the fibres spread at 90° to the first layer. A third layer is then added at 90° to the last. Three layers are the minimum, more may be added to produce a thicker felt. The wool is then thoroughly wetted with warm water. The mother felt and layered wool is then rolled around a large pole. This roll is wrapped in wet hides, tied up securely, and dragged behind a pair of horses, or a camel for a few hours.

When the bundle is unrolled the wool will

have felted into a strong mat about half an inch (1cm) thick. Any weak spots, or holes are patched with horsehair.

Food and Drink

The Mongolian's dietary requirements are almost entirely met by their flocks. The only food bought in is flour and rice. Vegetables are rarely eaten. The Mongols obtain all of the necessary nutrients by eating every part of the animal, nothing is wasted. Wild onions and garlic are sometimes used to season meat dishes.

During the summer months dairy products or white foods are eaten, comprising of cheese *byaslag*, butter, curds *aarts*, and the so-called yellow fat, or *örüm*, produced by boiling off the water from milk. Excess curds are pressed into cakes and dried on the roof of the *ger*. This dried form, called *aaruul*, will keep fresh almost indefinitely. Select cuts of raw meat, prepared during the summer are hung in the *ger* to produce *boorts* – dried meats for winter use.

During the winter months the animals do not produce milk, so the diet consists of fresh meat and the dried *aaruul* and *boorts*. The whole animal is eaten; only the skin and bone are left. Sheep are killed by making a small incision below the ribs and

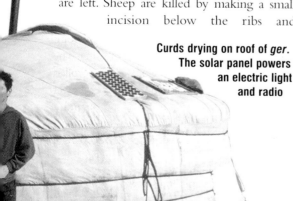

**Curds drying on roof of *ger*.
The solar panel powers
an electric light
and radio**

Airag-making in the *ger*

squeezing an artery; no blood is spilled and wasted. The blood is used to make sausages, similar to black pudding.

During summer the main drink is *airag*, fermented mare's milk. Inside every nomad *ger*, to the left of the door is a wooden frame supporting a sewn-up cow skin, or *khoohoor*, with the neck open and the shaft of a wooden paddle, or *booloor* sticking out. This is where the *airag* is fermented. Throughout the summer, milk is added and *airag* taken out in a continuous process. The fermenting *airag* must be stirred hundreds of times a day using the *booloor*. The drink is mildly alcoholic and has a very pleasant taste, even to the western palate. On a smaller scale, *airag* can be made in a wooden bucket, (metal or plastic are never used). A similar fermented milk drink made from camel's milk is treated with less respect and can be produced in a plastic barrel.

The nomads produce their own vodka or *aarkhi* by distilling *airag*. The distillation process is remarkably simple and takes just 30 minutes. The apparatus used is called a *burkheer*, consisting of a large pan of *airag* with a wide metal cylinder sitting just inside its rim. A round-bottomed pan of cold water sits on top of the cylinder and a small pan hangs inside. The whole apparatus sits on the stove. Alcohol evaporates and condenses on the base of the top pan, it then runs down

and drips into the small pan where it collects. Twenty pints (ten litres) of airag will produce four to six pints (two to three litres) of *aarkhi* of about 10% alcohol by volume. Further distillations will increase its strength.

Tea is drunk throughout the year. Chinese brick tea is used. Small pieces are broken off as required. Milk and salt are added to taste.

Recipes

Meat is often eaten in the form of *buuz* or steamed dumplings. These are popular throughout Mongolia, often eaten in huge numbers; ten per person is regarded as a minimum, at one sitting. They are usually eaten on their own, but on special occasions a Russian salad or pickled vegetables may also be served. A vegetarian version can be made using soya mince, or a similar meat substitute, Mongolians would always use meat.

RUSSIAN SALAD

Ingredients
- 6-8 potatoes
- 2-3 carrots
- 3-4 eggs
- 6 gherkins
- small tin of peas
- small onion
- 6 hotdogs
- 8oz mayonnaise
- 1 small turnip (optional)

Method
- Peel the potatoes, carrots, and turnip. Cut them into small cubes and boil for 15-20 minutes. Drain and leave to cool.
- Boil the eggs and cut into small cubes.
- Peel the onion and cut into small cubes.
- Cut the hotdogs into small cubes.
- Place the ingredients in a bowl and add the peas and mayonnaise and mix.
- Serve cold.

BUUZ

Ingredients

To make 20-30 dumplings: serves 3-4.

- 10oz (260g) plain flour
- 4oz (100ml) water, enough to make a non-sticky dough
- 1lb (450g) minced lamb
- 1 onion
- Garlic
- 3-5oz (80-120ml) cold water

Method

- Mix the flour and cold water in a bowl to make dough.
- Knead and roll the dough.
- Cut the dough into one inch (25mm) squares, and roll or press them into four inch (10cm) circles, slightly thicker in the middle than at the edge.
- Finely chop the onion and garlic. Mix with the lamb.
- Dissolve three teaspoons of salt in 3-5 oz (75 - 125 ml) of water. Add this to the mixture.
- Season with black pepper.
- Place 1-2 teaspoons of the mixture into the centre of each dumpling.
- Lift one point, then work in an anti-clockwise direction. Carefully lift the pastry over the meat, twisting and pinching as you go.
- Steam for 15-20 minutes.
- The dumplings are cooked when they are firm to the touch.

Variations on Buuz are:

Bansh:

The dumplings are boiled for 15-20 minutes in salted tea.

Huushuur:

These are three times bigger than *buuz* and flat, fried in oil or fat.

SÜÜTEI TSAI   salted tea

Ingredients

- Tea (unscented)
- Milk or cream
- 1-1½ teaspoons of salt

Method

Boil water in a pan with tea and salt. Green Russian tea is best, but any unscented tea will do. Add milk or cream and bring back to boil.

The shrine, or *Khoimar*, the sacred place at the back of every *ger*

Symbolism and cosmology

To the Mongolian people the *ger* is more than just a simple dwelling. In its construction the whole universe is represented. The roof represents the sky or vault of heaven. The *tono* is the sun and the entrance to the upper world. The *bagana* are the world tree by which one ascends to the upper world. In a trance-like state the Mongolian shaman actually enters the upper worlds through the *tono*.

Opposite the door at the northernmost part of the wall is the *khoimor*, the most honoured part of the *ger*. There is always a shrine here, usually with Buddhist images which share space with valued objects, family photographs, statuettes of the five animals, and in recent years, a portrait of Ghengis Khan.

Honoured guests are seated near the *khoimor*. Valued possessions, such as the *moorin khuur* (horse head fiddle), gun, horse bridle, decorated snuff bottle and smoking pipe are all stored close to the *khoimor*.

People sleep with their heads pointing North, towards the *khoimor*. This sleeping arrangement is reversed in Muslim countries where people sleep with the head pointing south, in the approximate direction of Mecca.

The hearth or *gal golomt* is sacred. In shamanic tradition it is the dwelling place of *Golomto*, daughter of *Tenggeri*, the father of heaven. The hearth contains the five basic elements of earth, wood, fire, metal, and water (metal in the grate and water in the kettle). The Buryat Mongols throw offerings onto the fire every morning. No rubbish is burned on the fire and outsiders should not take a light from it.

Setting up home

The family yurt is usually obtained as a gift from the bride's parents on a couple's marriage. A fairly basic new *ger* costs about US$600 – equivalent to a year's wages for a government run factory worker, a month's wages for someone working in the private sector, or the price of three good horses, 30 sheep, six camels or two cows. A good secondhand *ger* costs about US$300. Traditional painting can increase the price of a new *ger* to US$1000.

A large painted and carved *ger*, with floor, doors, and decorative cover can cost up to US$6000. The frame may last a lifetime; in Northern Mongolia where it is transported by ox cart just four or five times a year, a frame can last 70 years or more. In the Gobi Desert, where the flocks must be constantly moved as sparse pasture is used up and the *ger* is carried on the backs of camels, this constant moving and rough handling can reduce the frame's life to just 10 years.

The felt covers last about 10 years in Northern Mongolia. In the dryer climate of the Gobi Desert covers can last 20 years. Old and worn covers are used as additional insulation during the winter, and are overlain with newer felts. When they become too worn to use as covers at all they are used on the floor under the more decorative rugs.

The interior furnishings and seating arrangements are always the same. The altar is placed opposite the door at the back of the yurt. The hearth or stove is in the middle of the floor with firewood or other fuel in front and a low table behind. The western side is the domain of the men where male visitors and honoured guests sit and saddles, tools and *airag* (fermented mare's milk) are stored. The

Preparing to move home in the Gobi. The *ger* is taken down, leaving the household effects in place

women and children use the eastern side, where rugs, bedding, food, cutlery, crockery and water are stored. Servants, poor visitors and any sick or very young animals that need nursing, sit near the entrance *(fig 11)*. Both men and women work together in putting up and taking down the *ger*.

Etiquette

Traditionally, anyone stopping outside of a *ger* is invited in for a meal. A sheep is killed for the feast. When visiting a *ger*, the guest, whether known to the owner or not, simply walks in — to knock is to question the host's hospitality and is therefore impolite. However, it is wise to make sure the dog is under control before approaching. When entering the yurt it is considered impolite to touch the door frame or *busluur*. To stand on the threshold, or *bosgogh*, is considered the greatest insult, equivalent to stepping on the host's neck! The traditional greeting offered by the visitor consists of four questions: *are you well? is your family well? are your cattle/sheep fat? is the grass good?* The answer to each of these questions is *yes*, whatever the reality. After exchanging greetings the guest is offered tea, *airag* and then curds or other foodstuffs. Visitors to a Kalmuk yurt are offered *arkhi*; three glasses must be drunk in rapid succession. Following these formalities men exchange snuff and the party can become more relaxed. At the meal the guest carves and shares the meat.

Do's and don'ts in the ger

There are a number of rules which guests should follow in the *ger*.

Do
- Leave all weapons outside
- Take at least a little of any food or drink offered
- When offered *arkhi* or vodka, use the ring finger to flick a small amount to the sky, the wind and the earth before drinking
- Move around the *ger* in a clockwise direction

- Remove gloves before shaking hands
- Remove your hat before entering the *ger*

Do Not
- Step on the threshold
- Touch or lean on the *bagana*
- Point your feet at the hearth
- Put rubbish or water on the fire
- Bring sharp objects close to the fire
- Sit with your back to the altar
- Whistle
- Write in red pen
- Step over anyone, particularly older people
- Point a knife at anyone
- Sit with your feet out in front (kneel or sit cross legged)

The call of nature

There are no toilets on the Mongolian steppe, nor are there any bushes, trees, or rocks to hide behind. The traditional *del* allows one to stand or squat with its back spread to protect the wearer's modesty. It is polite to stand or squat at a reasonable distance from, and with one's back to, the *ger*. Before leaving the *ger* to relieve oneself, the euphemism of *mori kharakh*, or to 'look for a horse' is used.

Nomadism

The majority of Mongolian people still lead a nomadic life, moving home every month or two, literally to pastures new, as the grazing in an area becomes exhausted. Contrary to the popular view of nomadic life, the herdsman and his family do not just wander at random around the steppe. At any particular time of the year the Mongol family will be camped in the same place as their ancestors have camped for centuries. Before Ghengis Khan unified the many peoples of Mongolia during the 12th century, rivalry over grazing land caused endless fighting.

No one owns land in Mongolia. Over the centuries a system has evolved so that each family knows that it can move from pasture to pasture and find fresh grazing. Any family grazing its animals outside of its traditional range will be taking the livelihood from someone else.

The length of time a family stays in one place depends on the quality of pasture. In the Gobi Desert a typical family is forced to move ten times a year as the meagre vegetation is used up. The typical migration takes them 6–7 km, and they must move throughout the year.

In the more fertile Terelj region of Northern Mongolia a typical family need only move four times a year between summer pastures or *zuslan*. These migrations may be up to 60 km, but are usually less. During the winter (October to May) a number of families will live loosely together in sheltered valleys. These winter camps or *uvoljo* have permanent timber stabling for cattle, sheep and goats. The surrounding valley is left ungrazed until late autumn to supply winter

Ger **transport by Yak cart in Northern Mongolia**

feed. Cut hay is stored at the *uvoljo* to feed the stabled animals.

The *ger* takes about an hour to pack. In four hours the whole household is ready to move. The *ger* and all household effects are loaded onto carts, which are pulled by bulls or camels (never cows or horses). Some families dispense with the cart and carry the *ger* and effects directly on the backs of camels or yaks, particularly when moving over rough terrain. The new camp can be set up in an hour.

When de-camping, the *ger* is taken down first, leaving the household effects *in situ*. All furnishings and possessions are then conveniently in the open, from where they can be easily packed. The process of taking down the *ger* is carried out at a leisurely pace with plenty of time for tea breaks. However, the home is still packed and loaded in a remarkably short time.

Layout of *ger* interior

Wherever practical the *ger* is always pitched

with the door facing south. On the typical open steppe or desert of Mongolia this causes no problems. However, next to a cliff, forest, or closed valley, the yurt door will face the open country.

The south facing orientation ensures that the cold, prevailing wind from the north does not enter through the door. This same north wind draws smoke out through the open southern side of the *tono*. The sun shines into the back of the yurt throughout the day. The play of sunlight through the spokes of the *tono* casts light and shadows on the *bagana*

and the rear of the yurt by which every Mongolian can tell the time of day in any (south-facing) yurt.

Every aspect of life within the *ger* follows age-old traditions, from seating positions to the placement of furniture, to the filling of trunks and drawers. The *ger* interior is divided into different regions, each with its own practical use and/or spiritual significance. The major divisions delineate three regions: the men's side, the women's side and the khoimor or sacred space. There is no physical barrier delineating these regions, indeed the *ger* interior appears completely open. It is, therefore, important to familiarise oneself with *ger* layout and etiquette before visiting Mongol people in their home. Minor indiscretions by foreigners, however, are usually overlooked.

The hearth is at the centre of the *ger*, traditionally an open fire, now superseded by a metal stove. The fire is considered sacred, rubbish should not be burned on it, weapons should not be brought close to it, strangers should not take a light from it, and people should point the soles of their feet towards it. The stove opens to the eastern (women's) side. Behind the stove is a low table, on which food and drink are served. Fuel,

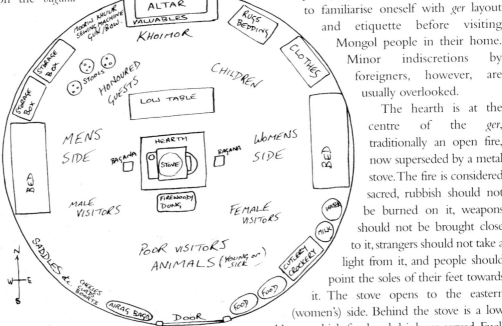

Fig. 11: Traditional layout of Mongolian *ger* interior

Traditional interior of a Gobi nomad *ger*

in the form of dried dung or wood is stored in front of the stove.

Within the *ger* the men's side is to the west and the women's to the east. On entering the *ger* men and women should walk directly to their own side, and sit in a position appropriate to their status. Servants, children, and beggars sit closest to the door. Honoured guests sit at the back of the *ger*, away from the door close to the *khoimor*. Casual visitors sit somewhere in between. When entertaining, the host sits to the rear (north) of the *ger* and to the east of the shrine.

At the north of the *ger* opposite the door is the *khoimor*. Religious objects, family photographs, and treasured objects are kept here, on a raised shrine. Before 1989 the *khoimor* was home to various communist medals and awards; these have now largely been superseded by portraits of the Mongolian national hero, Ghengis Khan. Other treasured possessions – a gun, a *Moorin Khuur* (horse-head fiddle), a sewing machine, a radio, and a clock – are usually found near the *khoimor*.

The household effects are stored in their own particular place around the walls. To the left of the door, on the men's side, is a large

wooden frame. This frame supports the *khoohoor*, a large leather bag made from a whole cow skin, for the preparation of Mongolia's national drink, *airag*, fermented mare's milk. Next to the *khoohoor* are bags containing *byaslag*, cheeses and *aarts*, curds, and at the top of the wall hang *boorts*, dried meats.

Moving clockwise around the walls, after the cheeses and dried meats are saddles, bridles and other horse accessories. A bed, doubling-up as a sofa occupies the western side and boxes containing clothing, and other personal effects sit between the bed and the *khoimor*.

Moving anticlockwise from the door, on the women's side are water containers and cooking utensils, followed by wooden buckets containing fermented drinks made from camel, goat and cow milk, as well as curds and cheeses. Another bed occupies the eastern side followed by more boxes containing the women's clothing, bedding and effects *(fig 11)*.

Felt rugs are placed on the floor, the best ones to the rear and older ones towards the door. Decorative rugs are sometimes hung

Modern *ger* interior

from the walls. Urban and tourist *gers* often have a decorative cloth hanging from the bottoms of the *uni* to cover the entire *khana*.

Religion

During the reign of the great khans in the 12th and 13th centuries, religions, including Islam, Christianity, Confucianism, and Buddhism, were embraced by the Mongolian people. Since the 16th century Tibetan Buddhism has been the major religion in Mongolia.

During the 1930s Mongolia's many Buddhist monasteries were destroyed and the monks either killed or sent to labour camps in Siberia. Religion was suppressed by the communist regime until 1989. Now some of the monasteries have been restored and Buddhism is again flourishing. Almost all *gers* contain a Buddhist shrine.

As well as Buddhism, other religious and quasi-religious beliefs are followed. Shamanism is practised throughout Mongolia, especially in the far north. A direct link between the spirit worlds and this are established through the medium of a shaman.

Ovoo worship is peculiar to Mongolia. An *ovoo* consists of a conical pile of stones, topped with upright sticks and brushwood. They are scattered throughout the country. Offerings, such as silk scarves, bones, money, crutches, bottles, or stones are placed on the *ovoo* and wishes are made. On passing an *ovoo* one walks to the left, or circles it three times in a clockwise direction. Any digging, hunting or woodcutting is prohibited near the *ovoo*.

An *ovoo*, a conical pile of stones, topped with upright sticks and brushwood

CHAPTER 4

The Mongolian *ger*

Urban *ger* in Ulaan Baatar

Cattle and sheep, like jewels
Glittering in the sun;
Mongolian tents, like buds,
Each ready to burst into bloom.
No smoke of war rises now on the beacon tower.
A rainbow floats in the eyes, a smile in the heart.

Liang Shang-ch'üan,
1955 (in Twitchet & Fairbank, 1991)

The Mongolians are the great nation of yurt dwellers; throughout the rest of central Asia its use has declined this century. Mongolia has continued using the yurt, or *ger*, as its primary form of housing, being home to at least 75 per cent of the population. Indeed, the Mongolian word *ger*, used to describe a yurt, actually means home. Traditionally there was no need for a separate word to describe the yurt, as every home was one.

Most towns in Mongolia consist of a small core of large buildings, factories and apartment blocks, a legacy of Russian occupation from the 1930s to 1989. These buildings are surrounded by large suburbs consisting of individual fenced compounds, each containing one or two yurts, which are home to most of the town's inhabitants. Even the capital, Ulaan Baatar, follows this model, with 40 per cent of the population living in some 50,000 *gers*.

Despite being effectively occupied by China for 200 years and Russia for 50 years, the Mongolian people have remained true to their traditional ways of life. Revolving around the rearing of livestock, a nomadic lifestyle, the *ger*, and the Buddhist or Shamanic religion. Outside of the capital the population still wears the traditional *del*, a long coat with a colourful sash around the waist worn by both men and women. The usual means of transport is the horse.

The winters are as cold as anywhere in the world, with temperatures regularly falling to -40°C. The average January temperature in Ulaan Baatar is -26°C. In springtime, strong winds of up to 60mph (96km/h) blow in from the north. Summer temperatures in the Gobi desert often reach 40°C. There is, however, little rain, the annual average rainfall is 12 inches (30cm). The sun shines for 260 days per year. The Mongolian *ger* is ideally suited to all of these climatic extremes.

The *ger*

The earliest complete yurt yet discovered was found in a 12th century grave in the Khentei mountains of Northern Mongolia. This yurt is remarkably similar in construction to the modern *ger*, with *khana* poles bent in the double curve common in the finest modern *gers*. A similar yurt burial, now housed in the Museum of Mongolian Culture in Ulaan Baatar and dating from the 14th century, shows the body covered with a complete folded *ger*. This *ger* has *khana* made from cleft wood, finished, probably with a drawknife, to give a square profile. The rods are 66 inches (1.67m) long with hole spacings of 5-6 inches (12-15cm). This would give a *ger* with a slightly lower wall, but otherwise indistinguishable from a modern nomad *ger*.

Mongolian *ger* maker fitting windows into the *tono*

During the eight centuries since these burials the design of the *ger* has changed little. Throughout Mongolia the *ger* follows an identical pattern of construction, with almost no regional variations. *Ger* frames are made by individual craftsmen, generally the same person makes and decorates every part of the frame, and often the furniture as well. There are also a few factories producing *gers*. These are low-tech consisting of a number of craftsmen working together. It takes a typical craftsman 15 days to make a complete 12 foot (3.5m) *ger* frame. Nomadic people always make their own covers and ropes using wool and hair from their own livestock. City dwellers often make their own covers using factory-made felt and a decorative cotton cover.

General description

The Mongolian *ger* always follows the same general pattern. The overall shape is one with a wall tapering inward slightly towards the top, with a low conical roof, topped with a smooth curve. *Gers* used as family dwellings are between 16 and 21 feet (4.9-6.4m) in diameter. The wall is always about five feet (1.5m) high. One of the main features inside the *ger* is a pair of ornate posts with a horizontal top piece which apparently support the *tono*. There is always a metal stove slightly forward of the centre.

The size of a *ger* is expressed in numbers of *khana*, the most usual sizes being four (14 feet [4.25m]) five (18 feet[5.5m]) and six *khana* (21 feet [6.4m]). Even the smallest *gers* never have less than three *khana*. A large 30 foot (9m) *örgöö* (palatial *ger*) has ten *khana*. Smaller yurts are often found alongside the family *ger*; these are typically 12 feet (3.7m) in diameter and are used as kitchens, dining rooms, workshops, or for storage.

Larger *gers* or *örgöö* of up to 30 feet (9m) in diameter, very occasionally larger, are often seen. These large *gers* were used as Buddhist temples towards the end of the Communist era. Many newly-rebuilt temples still have the *ger* which were used to keep the faith alive during more oppressive times. Now the large *gers* are more commonly used as restaurants, catering for foreign and Mongolian tourists, or for entertaining visiting dignitaries.

Khana

The *khana* follow a standard pattern throughout the country, the only exceptions being on unusually small or large *gers*. The only major differences are the degree of bending of the *khar mod* (poles) and the type of wood used. Wood

is either in the form of slats, or round poles.

Slats are usually of larch or occasionally birch, rectangular in section about 1½ x ½ inches (38x13mm), these are either machine-sawn and planed, or cleft and drawknifed smooth. The traditional craftsman goes to the forest to select and fell his trees, typically four or five larch trees of six inches (15cm) diameter are needed for each *khana*. In the forests of Northern Mongolia only about four per cent of trees are suitable, with straight knot-free trunks.

Round poles are usually coppiced willow, or occasionally birch saplings, ideally 1¼ inches (3cm) in diameter. The bark is always removed and the wood is sometimes, but not always, treated with animal fat as a preservative. Oversized round poles are shaved with a drawknife to give an octagonal or square profile of the required size. *Ger* makers and nomadic people acknowledge that round poles produce a lighter, stronger and more durable frame. City dwellers often prefer the more refined look and lower cost of slats.

The typical *khar mod* is 75-88 inches (1.9-2.25m) long, (*fig 12*)

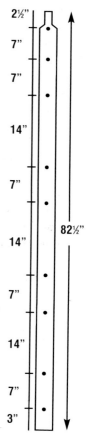

Fig. 12: Holes spaced on a typical Mongolian wall pole

2½"
7"
7"
14"
7"
14"
7"
14"
7"
3"

82½"

Ger maker with khana, showing bend in wall poles

with holes spaced 3-4 inches (75-100mm) from the bottom to the first hole, and 2½-3 inches (65-75mm) at the top. Crossovers/holes are spaced seven inches apart. On a 12 crossover rod a hole is drilled at each point except numbers 3, 6, and 9, counting from the bottom. On nine crossover poles numbers 3 and 7 are missed. The tops of slats are shaped to take the round *uni*.

The poles are usually bent to give the walls their typical profile. The simplest and most common bend consists of a single curve in the top half of the rod, leaving the tip 5-6 inches (12.5 -15cm) from its unbent position. A more elaborate profile uses the same curve with another small bend in the opposite direction near the top. The most elaborate curve: ideal, but less often used, consists of these two curves plus a slight opposite curve in the bottom half of the rod (*fig 13*).

The permanent bends are produced using water, heat and a blunt axe. Fifteen rods at a time are treated. They are soaked for a day and then heated for several hours. The heating is achieved in a long pit covered with sheet metal. The wet rods are placed in the pit and a fire, fuelled by dried animal dung, is lit at one end. The heat and smoke permeate the rods which become pliable whilst hot. The rods are taken out and hit once, in several places with a large, very blunt axe. This bends the rods, which are then held in their new form using wooden pegs driven into the ground. Once the rods have cooled and dried the bend is permanent.

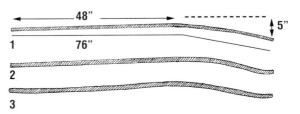

Fig. 13: Bends to give the khana its conical shape. 1. single bend, 2. double bend, 3. elongated 's' bend.

A typical *khana* has 15 *tolgoi* (heads), this requires 20 full-length *khar mod* as well as a number of shorter pieces to give a square end to the section. The rods always have their bottoms pointing to the left and their tops to the right.

Udeer

The *khana* rods are tied together using *udeer*: strips of wet rawhide, with holes cut close to either end. The free end passes through these slits to form a knot. As the rawhide dries, it shrinks, pulling the rods tightly together. The dry *udeer* are quite brittle and break easily, so there is a constant need for replacement (*fig 14*).

Bending wall poles using a blunt axe

Interlocking *khana* ends

Uni

The *uni* are the main feature distinguishing the Mongolian *ger* from any other type of yurt. These roof poles are a source of great pride to the yurt's owner. They are always straight and in all but the simplest *gers* they are highly decorated. The usual form of the *uni* has a round shaft for all but the top 25-30 inches (64-75cm). The top part is square in section and tapers from 1½x1½ inches (38x38mm) or 2x2 inches (50x50mm) at the shoulder, to between a half and one inch (13-25mm) square at the end (*fig 15*). Each top end fits into a mortise in the outer rim of the *tono*. The *uni* are painted red or orange and traditional patterns are painted or carved on the square section. The bottom end, or *bogs*, has two holes drilled in it about one and two inches (25mm and 50mm) from the end. String passes through these holes to form a loop or *sagaldarga*, which connects the *uni* to the *khana*. A simpler form of *uni* consists of a round pole of willow or birch, with a *sagaldarga* at one end and the other shaped to fit in the *tono*.

When asked "how big is your *ger*?" the Mongolian's reply will be, for example, six *khana*, eighty *uni*. There is one *uni* for each *tolgoi* (head). The number of *uni* fitting into the door frame is equal to the number of *khana* in the *ger*. Older *gers* often have a few *uni* missing due to breakage, but this does not significantly affect the overall performance of the *ger*. New *gers* often have spare *uni* standing either side of the entrance, giving a grand appearance rather like two flagpoles. As well as having aesthetic appeal, these two poles help the hold the cover tightly in place where it joins the door frame.

Tono

The *tono*, crown, roof-wheel, or 'eye of

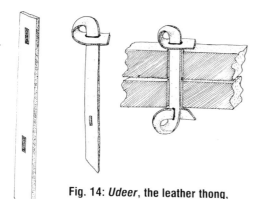

Fig. 14: *Udeer*, the leather thong, which joins the wall poles

Fig. 15: The straight *uni* or roof pole of the Mongol *ger*

heaven' forms the centre of the roof, the point through which light enters and smoke exits. It is the most elaborate and expensive single component of the yurt, and a distinctive feature unique to the Mongolian *ger*.

The *tono* is considered sacred: in shamanic tradition it represents the entrance to the upper world, it allows sunlight to enter and the smoke from the fire (also sacred) to escape. It is thus treated with great respect. When putting up the *ger* the *tono* should not be carried through the door, it is either placed in the

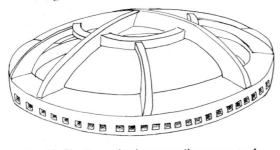

Fig. 16: The *tono*, also known as the crown, roof wheel and eye of heaven

middle of the *ger* before the walls are spread, or passed over the *khana*. The Mongolian *tono* is a large, fairly heavy (10-15kg), wheel made by a skilled carpenter. Within the outer wheel is a smaller circle, raised about eight inches (20cm) above the level of the rim on four *tsamkhraa* (curved spokes) which form a cross in the centre. There are four or six further *tsamkhraa* between the inner and outer circles *(fig 16)*.

The *tono* is painted red or orange and usually elaborately decorated with traditional

patterns. The finest *gers* have decorations carved into the timber of the *tono, uni, bagana* and door. This carving reflects the prestige of the owner and can increase the initial cost of the *ger* tenfold.

With the door closed the *tono* is the only source of natural light. The *ger* always faces south, so the regular diurnal movement of light and shadow around the yurt reflects the movement of the sun across the heavens. Thus the Mongol can tell the time of day in any yurt. During the winter, glass windows are fitted between the *tsamkhraa* to prevent heat-loss, while still allowing light to enter. A metal plate with a round hole between two *tsamkhraa* holds the flue-pipe upright and safely away from any flammable parts of the *ger*.

The *tono* rim is made from sections of timber, each forming one sixth or eighth of a circle. Two or three layers of these sections are laminated together to form a circle. The size of this circle depends on the diameter of the *ger*.

Ger Ø diameter	khana (no.)	tono Ø diameter	uni (no.)
13' (4m)	3 or 4	47" (120cm)	54
15' (4.5m)	4	51" (130cm)	66
16'6" (5m)	4	55" (140cm)	76
18' (5.5m)	5	59" (150cm)	81
21' (6.5m)	6	63" (170cm)	96

Mortises, square in section and pointing upwards at about 25°, are equally spaced around the outer edge of the rim. The top of

Tono in place

Raised *tono* allows smoke from an open fire to be drawn out of the *ger* by the prevailing wind. Rarely used since introduction of metal stoves

Carved *tono*. Good carving can increase the value of the *ger* tenfold

one *uni* fits into each of these mortises.

A less common arrangement of the roof has the *uni* permanently attached to the *tono* by dowels, which act as hinges. The whole roof frame is carried folded, in the form of a large cone, with the *tono* at the wide end. To put up the *ger*, the cone is placed upright in the middle. The *tono* is supported at the correct height by the folded *uni*; each pole is then unfolded from the centre and attached to the *khana*.

Before the introduction of the metal stove, open fires, often contained in a *tulga* (metal brazier) provided heat. The modern *tono* does not provide a very efficient means of venting smoke

from an open fire. The old-style *tono* had a centre raised up to two feet (60cm) above the rim. The windward side of this raised centre was covered with a felt *orkh*. The prevailing wind would produce a *venturi* effect to draw the smoke out.

In a new *ger*, a blue silk scarf with a few grains of rice knotted into it is hung from the *tono* to bring the new occupants luck. That they should prosper, like rice grains planted in the field (although the Mongols don't grow rice).

Chagata

The *chagata* is a steel loop, firmly attached to the centre of the *tono* to which a strong horsehair rope is attached. During fine weather this rope is tucked away as a sinuous curve between the *uni* and the cover. In the winter and spring, when high winds can be a problem, the rope is firmly attached to a water container, large stone or similar heavy weight. It is generally not pegged to the ground due to the Mongol taboo forbidding the disturbing of the earth.

Bagana

The central feature, unique to the Mongolian *ger*, is a pair of *bagana*; upright posts, each topped with a horizontal bar, which are tied to the underside of the *uni*. The 'T' piece at the top is usually reinforced with timber brackets. The *bagana* are generally decorated to match the *tono* and *uni*, and are of great cultural significance (*fig 17*). It is considered an insult to the host to lean against these posts.

In the Shamanic tradition the *ger* is regarded as a representation of the universe: the roof is the vault of heaven and the *tono* the entrance to the upper world. The *bagana* represent the world tree, which links this, and the upper worlds.

Fig. 17: Some typical varieties of *bagana* tops

A fine example of a carved *bagana* and its maker in Ulaan Baatar

Despite their appearance, they are not a structural necessity. *Bagana* are often loose and do not bear the weight of the *tono*. Indeed they almost hang from, rather than support the *tono*. They reduce the amount of free space within the yurt, which will stand perfectly well without them. This begs the question – why do most *gers* have *bagana*? There does not appear to be one simple answer. Tradition and culture are often stated reasons. But for nomadic families, who keep non-essential possessions to a minimum, they must also serve a practical purpose.

The roof of the Mongolian *ger* is much lower than other types of yurt to help retain heat and reduce the impact of high winds. It is conceivable that with a heavy covering of snow this low roof might collapse without the support of the *bagana*. The *ger* is very stable in continuous high winds, but sudden gusts, especially if they enter through the door, can distort the yurt and lift the roof.

The *chagata* rope attached to the *tono* centre is pegged to the ground, or tied to a heavy object in high winds. With this rope exerting a downward pressure and the *bagana* pushing upwards, the roof is held firm against any distortion.

The *bagana* are a great help when putting up or taking down the *ger*. The *tono* is easily supported by one person, while another fits or removes the *uni*.

Nars

The door is held in a *nars*, a sturdy frame with deep recesses in the outer edges of the uprights to accommodate the *khana* ends. These uprights are typically nine inches wide and have either metal loops attached or slots cut in

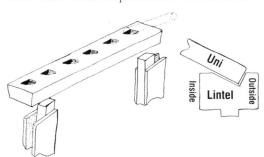

Fig. 18: Details of Mongolian door frame, or *nars*

them to which the *bushuur* (tension bands) are tied. The lintel or *totgo* has recesses in its top, in which the ends of the *uni* sit (*fig 18*). The bottom of the door or *bosgogh* is 4-6 inches (10-15cm) high and forms a distinct threshold to the *ger*. On entering one should always step

over the *bosgogh*; to step on it is considered a great insult to the host.

Khaalga

The Mongolian *ger* blurs the distinction between tent and building. The usual openness and insecurity of the tent does not apply to the *ger*, this is to a large extent due to the *khaalga* (door). In ancient times the door would have been a simple felt curtain, which is still used during the winter as an addition to the more elaborate wooden entrance. The *khaalga* of the modern *ger* is well made with timber panels. It can be locked as securely as any house door. The main door is a single one opening outwards to the left (when facing the *ger*). The finest *gers* also have a pair of double doors, opening inwards inside of the main door. The *khaalga* is usually decorated, often with the Mongolian national symbol of the endless knot, or with other traditional patterns.

Traditionally decorated door

Twrga

The cover of the modern *ger* consists of two distinct layers. The *twrga* (felt cover) was traditionally the only form of covering. Often the felt cover is now overlain with the *ger uhn boorees* (cotton cover). The *twrga* is now, as in ancient times, always of felt. Animal skins are never used. The felt is typically half an inch (12.5mm) thick on the walls and an inch (25mm) thick on the roof. A single layer of felt gives sufficient insulation for summer use. To give protection from the harsh Mongolian winters up to five further layers are added.

The *twrga* consists of a number of individual large overlapping felt mats. The roof cover is made from two or three parts called *deever* which overlap each other. The lower edge of the *deever* reaches down as far as the shoulder of the *ger*. The wall covers are in two or three overlapping parts consisting of rectangles fifteen feet (4.6m) long and slightly wider than the wall is high (about 5'6" [1.65m]). These rectangles have securing ropes attached to the two top corners.

The *deever* are shaped to leave a circular hole around the *tono*. If they do not form a good fit, an additional square of felt called the *burees*, with a more accurate circle cut into it is placed on top. The roof hole has a cover, the *örkh*, consisting of a square of felt with a rope at each corner. At night or in heavy rain the *örkh* covers the crown completely. During the day one of the securing ropes is untied and the front half is pulled back to admit light through the south-facing part of the *tono*.

Felt (esgi) is made by beating and

Elements of *twrga* (felt cover)

Wall felt - *twrga* (3 pieces for 20' ger)

Roof felt - *deever* (2 or 3 pieces)

Crown cover - *örkh*

Crown hole cover - *burees* (not always used)

Fig 19: Felt (*esgi*) components of the *ger* cover

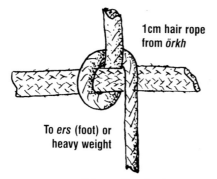

1cm hair rope from *örkh*

To *ers* (foot) or heavy weight

2-3cm x ½cm *busluur*

Fig. 20: Knots in horsehair ropes used to secure *ger* cover

one piece. Less common, but more practical outer covers are made from waterproof, Russian-made canvas. These covers are sewn from overlapping strips, which shed the rain (*see chapter 9*).

Busluur and securing ropes

The *twrga* and *ger uhn boorees* are held firmly in place by horsehair ropes or *busluur*. These ropes are made by the *ger* owner who plaits a number of hair cords together to produce a flat rope or tape about an inch (25mm) wide and ¼ inch (12.5mm) thick. Two or three cords are pulled tightly around the walls and secured to special loops, or slots in the door frame. At least four ropes hold the roof felts in place. These are tied to the *busluur* and are either attached to heavy stones or to the wooden floor, if fitted. Shamanic taboos forbid disturbance of the earth, so pegs are not driven into the ground (*figs 20 and 21*).

rolling layered wet sheep fleece. The felting process turns the wool into a thick, strong mat, with excellent insulating properties. Natural oils give the felt a degree of waterproofing, sufficient for the dry climate of central Asia. The basic felt is made in mats about four by eight feet (1.2x2.4m). Two or three people working together can make up to four of these felts in a day. Each of these mats uses four fleeces. The individual felts are sewn together to make the *twrga* and *deever*. It takes about 100 fleeces and two weeks to make an entire *ger* cover (*fig 19*).

Ger uhn boorees

The modern *ger* is still covered with felt in the traditional way. An additional outer cotton cover, or *ger uhn boorees*, usually covers the felt. This is usually a purely decorative layer made from white cotton, which is not waterproof and is more flammable than felt. These decorative covers are made from interlocking triangles of cloth (*see chapter 11*). Unlike the felt covers the *gher uhn boorees* it is made in

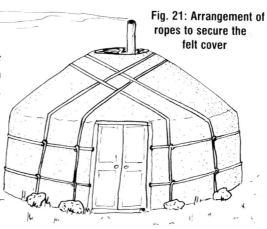

Fig. 21: Arrangement of ropes to secure the felt cover

Heating

There were once three boys called a fat boy, a butter boy and a straw boy. One day, a wind blew and it closed an airing panel of their ger by blowing over its covering flap. The straw boy went out in order to open the flap, but the wind blew him away. After him the fat boy went out, but a dog caught him and swallowed him. The butter boy was afraid to go out and melted away sitting beside his open fire in his roasting hot ger. And that was the end of the three boys.

Mongolian Folk tale (Damdinsuregyn)

The *zuukh*, a metal stove, kept constantly alight to cook, and heat the *ger*. Dung for fuel in front of the stove

Traditionally heat was provided by a fire contained in a steel basket-type brazier, or *tulga*. Smoke found its way out through a raised *tono*, helped by the prevailing north wind. The *tulga* and raised *tono* are no longer in common use.

At the centre of every modern *ger* is the *zuukh*; a stove made from sheet steel, supported on three stones. Traditionally these stones represent the host, the hostess and the daughter-in-law, mother of the heir. The fireplace is referred to as the ancestral hearth and is treated with great respect. The *zuukh* is made from thin sheet steel, and weighs less than 10kg. Practicality, and efficiency of the design more than compensates for any shortcomings in quality of materials and manufacture.

The typical stove consists of a box, square or round in section, about 18x18x18 inches (45x45x45cm). There is a small door in the front, opening to the eastern, or women's side of the *ger*, which is used to add fuel and to control the air supply. At the rear is a smaller steel box from which the flue-pipe projects. Hot flue gases pass through this box, radiating much of their heat into the *ger*, rather than wasting it up the chimney. A circular lid fits into a 15 inch (38cm) hole in the top of the stove. The lid is removed to light the fire and to sit cooking pots in the aperture. The stove is kept alight continually during the winter months, making the *ger* a warm haven from the bitter cold outside (*fig 22*).

The fuel for the stove depends on the local terrain. In the north of Mongolia the extensive Taiga forests provide ample firewood. In Ulaan Baatar and other cities coal is used. However, most of Mongolia consists of treeless steppe or

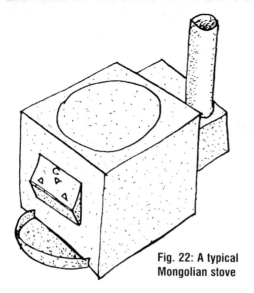

Fig. 22: A typical Mongolian stove

coloured except, occasionally, for a red border. Factory-made Chinese or Russian synthetic pile carpets are also used.

When the *ger* is pitched at the more permanent winter camp or *uvolgo,* a wooden floor is often added. Town dwellers' and tourist *gers* usually have wooden floors. The floor is typically made from larch planks in nine sections which fit together to form a circle about a foot (30cm) wider than the *ger (fig 23).* The floor is supported clear of the ground on wooden bearers. During the winter the join between the cover and the floor is protected by wooden billets about ten inches (25cm) long, which are tied edge-to-edge around the base of the walls. Earth or stones perform the same purpose on poorer *gers.*

Tourist *gers,* which do not need to be mobile, often have concrete floors with one or two doorsteps. Steel loops or posts are set into the concrete to secure the yurt. The tourists are as often as not Mongolians from the city wishing to return, for a short time at least, to their nomadic roots.

desert, where the only fuel is dried animal dung. This is collected throughout the year using a willow basket, or *arag,* which is slung over the shoulder. A wire, hand-shaped tool on a short pole is used to flick the dung into it. Horse dung makes the best fuel; camel, cow and yak burns fairly well, sheep and goat droppings are small but can be burned if nothing else is available.

Floor

The earth floor of the *ger* is always covered. Traditionally felts were used, worn out *ger* covers were placed next to the ground with better quality felt rugs on top. The modern nomad yurt often has a floor covering of linoleum, tough PVC sheeting or similar material, overlain with rugs. The traditional Mongol felt rugs are about three by six feet (1x2m), sewn through with traditional patterns using thick woollen thread. These rugs are not

Fig. 23: Arrangement of timbers for floor of a Mongol *ger*

CHAPTER 5

Other yurt types

The bentwood yurt *oba, öy or ûq*

This type of yurt differs significantly from the Mongol *ger*, although most of the basic principles are the same. Here is a brief overview.

The bentwood yurt has roof poles or *ûq* bent to form a curve at the roof-wall junction, producing a profile more rounded than the Mongol *ger* (*fig 24*). This yurt-type is used throughout the region formerly known as Turkestan, stretching from Eastern Turkey to

Fig. 24: Bentwood yurt, with its lighter crown and bent roof poles, used from Turkey to China

Northern China, with its stronghold in Kazakstan, Kirgistan and Uzbekistan. As with the Mongol *ger*, the Turkic words *oba, öy or ûq* used to describe the yurt actually mean 'dwelling'.

The crown *düynük* or *çevlik* is constructed from two or three lengths of wood steam-bent and joined to form a circle. The raised centre is made from thin willow rods or wooden laths. Mortises in the crown pass right through the rim, so that the roof pole ends project slightly into the space in the middle. This type of roof-wheel is much lighter than the *tono* of the Mongolian *ger*.

The bottom two or three feet of each roof pole bends in a gentle curve, so that the end is at an angle of about 35-50° to the main body of the pole. The top six inches (15cm) or so of the roof poles are tapered to fit through the crown mortises. This taper often has a shoulder to stop it pushing through too far. Each roof pole is attached to the wall by strings, which must be individually tied to each *khana* (or *terim* in Turkic) head. The wall poles are usually bent with a uniform curve along the entire length. A more elaborate double elongated 'S' shaped curve is sometimes used.

As with the Mongolian *ger*, the usual covering material is felt. However, in a hot climate the walls may be made from reed mats to allow air to circulate. The felts are often decorated with inlays of different coloured wool. The tension bands are wider than in the Mongolian *ger*, as the outward pressure is greater with no *bagana* to support the crown. This band is usually highly decorated.

Two tiered yurt *hâne, hïrgâ*

The two-tiered yurt is used in Afghanistan, where it is known as the *hâne, hirgâ* or *hâna-yi hïrgâ*. The wall poles are short, so that each *khana* is only half as high as the wall. Two *khana* are stacked one on top of the other to give the wall its full height. From the outside of the covered yurt this two tiered structure is not apparent. These yurts often have very tall pointed roofs. This more complex construction may make for easy transport by donkey (although the roof poles are still very long). Or it may be the result of a lack of sufficient long poles to make normal full-height *khana (fig 25)*.

For a full account of the bentwood, and two-tiered, yurts, refer to *Nomad Tent Types of the Middle East*, by Peter Andrews (1997).

Modern yurts

Travellers from Western Europe have described yurts for centuries. Marco Polo and Carpini described them in the 13th century. Fr. Evarist Huc, in his *Travels in Tartary, Thibet and China*

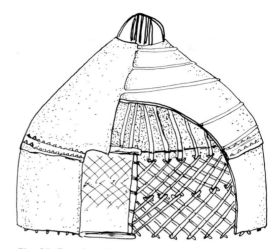

Fig. 25: Two tiered yurt. Low wall trellises are stacked one on top of the other. Used in Afghanistan

An English-made bentwood yurt

Modern US yurt made by Nesting Bird Yurts (Photo courtesy of Nesting Bird Yurt Company. Photo: Dave Scheifelbein)

(1844-6) described yurts as looking like balloons about to take flight. The British army encountered yurt dwellers in Northern Afghanistan in the late 19th century. Despite this contact the yurt was not adopted in the West until its gradual appearance in North America in the late 1960s. Inspiration, apparently, came from an article by William Douglas in the March 1962 issue of *National Geographic*. The photographs in this article had a wide influence, inspiring my own interest in yurts. The Indian army made copies, using these pictures, to house their officers in the war against Pakistan in the harsh climate of the Himalaya.

American yurt design rapidly moved away from the traditional pattern. Two early yurt

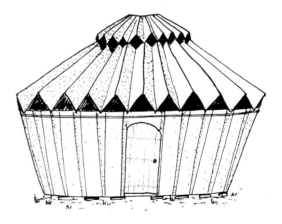

Fig. 26: Copperthwaite yurt. Made from plywood, a popular yurt-inspired form of self-build housing used in the USA since the 1970s

designers were Aaron Faegre and Bill Copperthwaite. Aaron Faegre used a wooden trellis wall. The laths were joined with rivets or bolts. There were no shorter pieces to square the *khana* ends so joining two sections together involved numerous nuts and bolts. The roof was made using rods connected to form a conical trellis, so no crown was needed. Details of this design can be found in **Shelter** (1973) or **Structure Constructor** (1997).

The Bill Copperthwaite design is a yurt-shaped building which is not portable. It has solid timber walls which slope outwards and a folded steel roof. These dwellings are a popular form of self-build housing in the United States *(fig 26)*.

There are currently a number of commercial yurt-making companies in the US who produce well made heavy-duty yurts with Douglas fir or similar frames and PVC covers. They take up to a day to erect and are used as homes, ski and hunting lodges, studios etc. The wall laths are joined using rivets, with hole spacings of up to sixteen inches. The tension band is replaced by a high-tensile steel cable, which passes between each crossover of the *khana* head. Roof poles do not connect directly to the *khana* but have a slot in the end, which fits over the tension cable. The crown consists of an open wheel, with no spokes, topped with a clear plexiglass dome.

Borealis Yurts have an interesting roof construction: five main roof rafters join at the centre. Once these are up, cross-pieces are fitted between them to give the appearance of a pentagonal crown. Further roof poles of varying length then fit between these cross pieces and the *khana*.

There are currently several professional yurt makers working in the UK, including myself. We produce fairly authentic Mongol and bentwood yurts, using English hardwoods. Covers are of cotton canvas. Yurts, either Mongolian or bentwood, are popular in the UK among people from all backgrounds and social classes. They are used as summerhouses, for camping, as student accommodation and workshops, for retreats, classrooms, saunas and places of worship, for weddings and parties. They are a popular form of dwelling amongst new age and travelling people, many of whom build their own.

PART TWO
YURT CONSTRUCTION

**Sixteen foot mongol *ger* frame made in English ash
by Woodland Yurts**

CHAPTER 6

Build your own yurt

The following pages tell you all you need to know to build your own yurt

What type of yurt to build?

Before starting you will need to decide whether you want a Mongolian *ger* or a bentwood yurt. The level of skill required is about the same for each type. The weekend yurt described in chapter 12 is the simplest form, ideal for absolute beginners. Each type has certain advantages and disadvantages.

YURT TYPE	ADVANTAGES	DISADVANTAGES
WEEKEND YURT	Simple construction	Small size
	No special skill or expensive tools needed	Low wall and door
	Quick to make	Too small for safe use of a woodburning stove
	Inexpensive	
	Extremely portable	
	Plenty of room for two people or a small family	
MONGOLIAN GER	Very robust structure	Joinery skills needed
	Steam bending not essential	Power tools make construction easier
	Bagana can be fitted to aid stability in extreme weather	Lower effective wall height than bentwood yurt
	Cover simple to make	
	Less wastage of wood	
BENTWOOD YURT	Greater effective wall height	Steam bending necessary
	Lighter crown	Wastage of timber due to breakout, knots etc.
	Fewer power tools needed for construction	Slightly more difficult cover manufacture
	More rustic appearance	Larger crown and bentwood poles less easy to transport

How long will it take?

This is obviously a difficult question to answer. A skilled woodworker with a fully equipped workshop will need about 70 hours to make a ten foot *ger* and cover. A complete beginner with the minimum of essential tools might take 100 hours. A 16-foot yurt will take about 50 per cent longer, so 110–150 hours will be needed. A beginner should be able to make a weekend yurt frame in about 18 hours. The cover will take a further 18 hours.

The Mongolian *ger* and the bentwood yurt take about the same length of time to make. The bentwood roof poles take longer to make than straight ones, but the simple crown construction saves time.

Necessary skills

The most important quality in the first-time yurt builder is patience and perseverance. Viewing the whole process of construction can be a bit daunting, so proceed one stage at a time. Each stage is quite simple and finishing the *khana* (for example) gives a huge incentive to carry on and make the roof. A basic knowledge of woodwork and the use of a sewing machine are a distinct advantage, but by no means essential. Absolute beginners, with no practical experience whatsoever have made very fine yurts, of both Mongolian and bentwood construction. Indeed, the sense of achievement at finishing the yurt is infinitely greater for the beginner.

Essential tools

- Good, sharp handsaw
- Electric jig-saw
- Curved knife
- Electric drill
- ⁷⁄₁₆" (4.5mm) drill bit
- 1" (25mm) wood drill bit
- Sliding bevel
- G-cramps (at least four)
- Workbench
- Smoothing plane
- Sewing machine
- Cigarette lighter

Useful tools

This list includes the tools, which, though not essential, make the job easier and/or neater.

- Electric planer
- Bench drill press
- Band-saw
- Dust extractor
- Surform plane
- Steam wallpaper stripper
- Small butane blow-torch
- Spokeshave
- 4 inch (100mm) Ø Plastic pipe (7 feet [2m] long)

Materials

Here is a list of the typical requirements for a ten foot *ger*; more exact lists of timber and canvas requirements are given with the worked examples.

- Wall rods, 5 feet (150cm) long (70)
- Roof poles, 5 feet 3 inches (158cm) (32)
- 1¼ inch (30mm) thick timber (1m²)
- 4mm nylon braided cord (75m)
- Waterproof canvas (35m²)
- Plastic-coated canvas (2m²)
- Rope (30m)
- Wood glue
- Linseed oil (one pint [500ml])
- Strong thread to sew cover
- Brass eyelets (grommets) (60)
- Screws (1 inch No.6) (30)

Canvas

Obviously, the bigger the yurt, the more canvas you will need to cover it:

Yurt diameter	Canvas requirements (sq m)
8' (2.4m)	28m²
10' (3m)	35m²
12' (3.7m)	48m²
14' (4.27m)	60m²
16' (4.8m)	75m²

CHAPTER 7

Frame construction

Basic techniques

The following techniques apply to any size or type of yurt; any deviation from the basic technique is described in the worked examples.

How much wood will it take?

Before preparing the wood, decide exactly what size and type of yurt you want to build. Make sure you have enough rods of the right dimensions. Roundwood wall and roof poles should be about an inch in diameter. Sawn timber wall rods can be in slats, typically 1¼ x ¾ inches (32x19mm) or ½ x 2 inches (13x50mm), or square in section ¾ x ¾ inches (19x19mm). Roof poles need to be square in section at least 1¼ x 1¼ inches (32x32mm). The number of wall poles needed depends on the size of the yurt. For a ten foot yurt you will need about 75 rods, while a 16 footer uses about 110.

The wall height depends on the length of the individual wall poles:

Length of wall pole	Wall height
4'6" (135cm)	3'6" (105cm)
5' (150cm)	4' (120cm)
5'9" (173cm)	4'6" (135cm)
6'6" (2m)	5' (150cm)

Generally the roof poles measure about half of the diameter of the *ger*, slightly longer for bentwood yurts. The number of roof poles is equal to the number of *khana* heads, plus four. With nine inch (23cm) hole spacing this is equal to the circumference in feet, plus four. So a 10 foot (3m) diameter (30 foot [9m] circumference) yurt will need 34 five foot (150cm) roof poles and a 16 footer (4.9m) will need 54 eight foot (2.4m) poles.

The worked examples later in this book give exact numbers for specific yurts.

Preparing the wood

The wood will probably arrive rough-sawn or as green poles with the bark on; either way it will need preparation. The first job is to sort through and discard any rods which are too bent, or have a number of knots or splits. Rods with a single knot or other imperfection can be used to make the shorter *khana* end pieces. The rods can now be cut exactly to length.

The *khana* has a large number of short pieces making up its square ends; rather than cutting these to length now it is easier to make extra full-length rods and cut them to length once they have been drilled and finished. For really neat holes it is

Wall poles: Measure around any large curves

Ignore 'dog-legs'

Roof poles: Measure straight line between ends

Fig. 27: Measure bent wall rods around the curve, ignoring any dog-legs. Measure a straight line between the two ends of roof poles

worth drilling them before stripping the bark or planing, so that any rough edges are removed.

Roundwood

The choice of wood for your first yurt will probably be decided by what is available locally. If you live near a coppice woodland, roundwood poles are inexpensive or even free, and easy to work. They give a strong and attractive yurt with an individual and rustic character.

Many local Wildlife Trusts coppice at weekends. They are always looking for volunteers, and are glad to let you take some of the cut rods home, in exchange for a day's cutting. Or find a farmer who grows willow as a biomass crop; rods will cost about 50p each.

Greenwood poles should be cut during the winter months, when the wood contains less sap and will be more durable. More importantly, both nature conservation in the woodland and the lifespan of the trees will be enhanced. Cutting wood during the summer can disturb nesting birds and other wildlife. Young shoots, which re-grow from the cut stump, will not have matured enough to survive frosts during the following winter.

Curved poles and 'dog-legs' need special care in cutting to length. Measure around the curve of slightly bent wall poles. Measure a straight line between the ends of bent roof poles. Ignore dog-legs when measuring. Bent and twisted poles will not make a good yurt (*fig 27*).

The poles can be left natural, with the bark on, or stripped for a light, attractive finish. Drill the rods before stripping the bark. Use an inward-curving knife to remove bark. Round off the ends of the poles using a sharp knife or surform tool.

The stripped poles can be treated with boiled linseed oil to give an attractive and durable finish. Apply the oil liberally with a cloth, leave to soak for several hours and wipe off the excess. More coats can be applied for a better finish.

Tie the wall rods together soon after cutting, so that slightly bent poles can pull each other straight as they dry. If you are storing the rods before use, tie them into tight bundles, again, so that they dry straight.

Sawn timber

If you live in an urban area or near a sawmill, sawn timber will be easier to obtain. This requires slightly more work but will give an attractive, strong frame with a more refined character. The cost can be astronomical, so shop around. You may be lucky enough to find suitable offcuts for little or no cost.

Cheap or free timber comes in many forms: I found a maker of oak timber floors who cut the edges off of planks before processing. These offcuts made perfect yurt rods. An hour rummaging through his scrap pile would give me one or two yurts worth for just £10. The same timber cut to order would have cost about £300. One of my early yurts was made from a batch of factory-reject broom handles, bought from a car boot sale for £15. Another fine yurt was made from discarded tobacco crates, made from mahogany!

The timber must be straight-grained and knot-free. Hardwoods are better than softwoods. Ash is probably the best timber to use for the wall and roof poles. Beech and oak are also excellent. The wood for the walls and roof poles can be used green (unseasoned). The wood for laminated crowns must be thoroughly seasoned, or kiln-dried. Beech, oak and maple are very good.

Softwoods are weaker, and do not steam bend very well. However, larch is the timber most commonly used in Mongolia, so it does produce a perfectly good *ger*. The Mongols' choice of larch is probably dictated more by the flora of the Taiga forest than by a preference for that particular wood. Douglas fir and red cedar are also suitable.

Sawn timber will need to be planed to give a smooth finish. A hand plane is fine, but hard work. An electric planer is quicker, but extremely noisy. Plane all four sides. Remove sharp edges with the plane, drawknife or

sandpaper. Round the ends with a surform tool. Finish with boiled linseed oil.

Drilling wall poles

The felt-covered Mongolian *ger* has holes spaced at about seven inches (17.5cm) apart to produce an extremely robust, but heavy, yurt. With a canvas cover the frame can be more open with nine or 12 inch (23 or 30cm) spacing. Wider gaps produce a more delicate, but lighter yurt using less timber.

For this example we will assume a nine-inch (23cm) spacing, and five foot (150cm) rods. Drill seven ³⁄₁₆ inch (4.5mm) holes, exactly nine inches (23cm) apart in each rod. Leave two inches (50mm) over at one end and four (100mm) at the other. If using poles of a different length keep the nine-inch spacing but drill more or less holes, as appropriate. If you are using roundwood poles, and will not be steam-bending them, it is possible to use the natural bend, present in

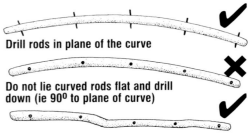

Drill rods in plane of the curve

Do not lie curved rods flat and drill down (ie 90° to plane of curve)

Drill rods at 90° to dog-legs. Ignore these when measuring

Fig. 28: Drill bent poles in the same plane as the curve, or at 90° to dog-legs

most poles to your advantage. To do this, drill the rods in the same plane as the curve (fig 28). When the *khana* are assembled, the rod ends should be pointing slightly towards the inside of the yurt, giving the same effect as steam bending. If you are using a hand-held electric drill the easiest way to space the holes is to make a fixture:

Take a piece of hardwood 12 inches (30cm) long. Hammer a 4mm nail through the wood about two inches from one end. The nail should go right through and with the point protruding about an inch. Drill a ³⁄₁₆ inch (4.5mm) hole exactly nine inches (23cm) from the nail. After drilling the first hole in each rod, place the nail in it. Now use the hole in the fixture as a guide to drill the second hole. Repeat for the other five holes (fig 29).

sticks out too far cut the end off with a hacksaw). Now mark a point exactly nine inches (23cm) along from the protruding nail. Fix this piece of wood securely to the drill table so that the drill just enters the wood at the marked point. Make a mark two inches (50mm) from this hole (towards the nail). To drill the rods; line up the top end of the rod with the two inch mark. Drill through the middle of the rod, now fit this hole over the protruding nail and drill the second hole, continue until all of the holes are drilled. If your rods are all of sawn timber of exactly the same width it is worth putting a nail behind the drill hole in the fixture to ensure that each hole is exactly central (fig 30).

Fig. 29: Simple fixture to ensure accurate spacing of holes when using a hand-held electric drill

If you are using a bench or pillar drill-press:
Take a flat piece of timber two or three feet (60-90cm) long and three inches (75mm) wide. Mark a point in the middle of its width and two thirds of the way along its length. Hammer a 4mm (or thereabouts) nail through it, so that the point projects about an inch (if it

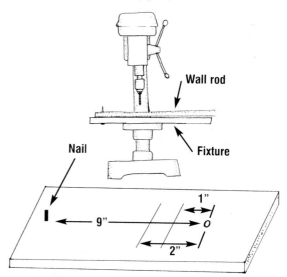

Fig. 30: Fixture for accurate hole spacing using a bench or pillar drill

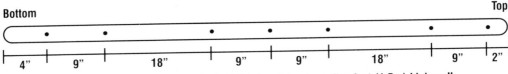

Bottom   **Top**

| 4" | 9" | 18" | 9" | 9" | 18" | 9" | 2" |

Fig. 31: Hole spacing in a 78 inch (2.05m) rod, to give a five foot (1.5m) high wall

If you are leaving undrilled crossover points you will need to make up a template by marking out a wall rod and drilling it at the appropriate points. Hold this template in place on top of one of the undrilled rods and drill the first hole. Now push a nail through the hole to hold the rods in place. Drill the other holes (*fig 31*). If using thin slats of sawn timber you can stack two or three and drill them together to save time.

Drilling roof poles

For a roundwood yurt drill a hole at one and two inches (25 and 50mm) from the bottom end of each roof pole. For a typical sawn timber *ger* these holes should be ¾ and 1½

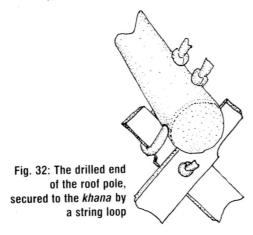

Fig. 32: The drilled end of the roof pole, secured to the *khana* by a string loop

inches (19 and 38mm). The holes need to be drilled at 45° to the required plane of the pole: stand with the main body of the pole to your right, decide how you want the pole to sit, turn it ⅛ of a turn away from you and drill straight down (*fig 32*).

Joining *khana* rods

Traditionally the wall rods always rise from the left at the bottom to the right at the top.

Wet rawhide is the traditional material for joining the *khana* rods. This is unpleasant to handle and prone to breakage when dry. Even brand-new Mongolian *gers* usually have a few broken *udeer*. Luckily modern nylon braided cord is ideal for the job: cheap, easily available, and durable.

Cardoc J cord or similar braided nylon, about ⁵⁄₃₂ inches (4mm) thick is ideal. For a more authentic look, use brown nylon cord, such as shoelaces. Use leather shoelaces for an (almost) authentic *ger*. The ends should be burned, rather than cut, to prevent fraying. A disposable lighter is a good tool for the job. A small butane blowlamp is even better.

Take a piece of cord about 15 or 20 feet (4–6m) long. Form one end into a hard 'needle' by heating the first inch or so and rolling it between your fingers (beware of the obvious risk of burning yourself). Now tie a knot in the other end and pass the string through two adjacent holes. Pull it as tight as you can. A strong thumbnail is useful to lock the string in place while you tie a knot securing the two rods together as tightly as possible. If one knot does not pull the cord tight enough, tie another knot behind the first.

A useful addition is a guide string around the *khana* to indicate exactly how wide it needs to be spread: calculate the exact horizontal distance between knots to give the required diameter. To calculate the gap, divide the yurt circumference, minus the door width by the total number of gaps between heads.

Knot distance =

circumference minus door width

(divided by) number of gaps

Tie the guide string around the *udeer* (*khana* connecting string) between the two overlapping rods at each second knot down. Pull the string tight and measure the spacing as you go.

The door

The simplest and most portable door frame for your yurt consists of two uprights of willow or hazel 1½-3 inches (38-75mm) in diameter and as long as the door is high. These are tapered at each end to fit into 1 inch (25mm) holes drilled into the top and bottom of the frame. The top and bottom consists of lengths of the same wood about three inches (75mm) in diameter and three feet (91cm) long drilled at two inches (50mm)

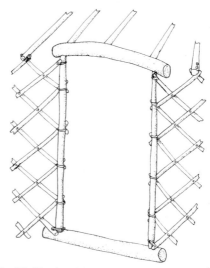

Fig. 33: Simplest frame made from roundwood poles

from either end to take the tapered ends of the uprights. The top part of the frame is drilled to take three or four of the roof poles. The door consists of a canvas curtain, weighted at the bottom and hung from brass hooks (*fig 33*).

A more elaborate and weatherproof, but less portable door can be made with a solid timber frame, fitted with a double or single door. The door is traditionally elaborately carved or painted. This door can be made in its own separate frame, which can be fitted to the front of the yurt door-frame when required.

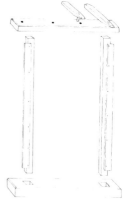

Fig. 34: Door frame made from sawn timber

Steam bending

The permanent bending of roof and wall poles may, at first, seem a daunting prospect. However, the process is quite simple, and not particularly time-consuming. The domed roof of the bentwood yurt and the inward sloping walls of the Mongolian *ger* are a result of steam bending. Mongolian *gers* are often made without any bentwood, giving parallel walls curving slightly inwards at the middle. This does not adversely affect the performance of the yurt. For a bentwood yurt steam-bending of the roof poles is essential.

Before you start you will need to construct a steam-box. The box must be waterproof on the inside and insulated to prevent heat loss. The simplest steam box can be made from a four-inch plastic gas-pipe or soil-pipe, wrapped in insulating material with a loose fitting wooden plug at each end. A piece of hose-pipe is pushed through one of these plugs to supply steam (*fig 35*).

Make sure that the steam can escape, either around the loose plug or through a hole in the pipe or plug. A completely sealed steam box will explode!

A more elaborate steamer can be easily constructed from waterproof plywood lined with insulating material and plastic. Beware of making the steam-box too big, or it will never heat up. It is better to do a few rods at a time than waste hours trying to heat all of the rods at once.

An electric steam wallpaper stripper is the easiest way to ensure a constant and plentiful supply of steam. Push the end of the steam pipe through the end plug of the steamer. The water level will need topping up about every hour.

If you do not have access to electricity,

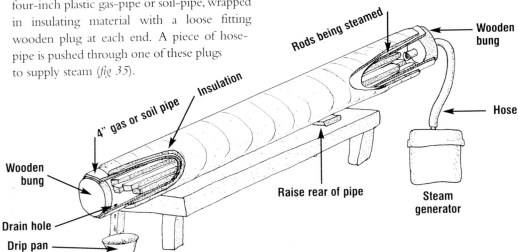

Fig. 35: Simple steam box made from plastic drain or gas pipe. Steam supplied from electric wallpaper stripper

steam is easily supplied by a pressure cooker with the valve removed, or a large kettle, kept boiling on a paraffin stove, a portable gas ring, or an open fire. A plastic pipe takes steam from the kettle to the steam box.

It is important that the wood to be bent is straight-grained. The bend is likely to fail where the grain has been cut. The rods will need to be steamed until they are heated right through and are flexible. For wall rods about thirty minutes will be sufficient. Thicker roof poles or bentwood crowns will need longer.

Once the rods are steamed you must work fast. The wood remains flexible for a very short time. The rods are hot, wear gloves. Take rods from the steamer one at a time and force them into the former (figs 36 & 56). Once the rods are in the former leave them to cool completely, ideally overnight. The rods will take a few days to completely set in their new shape. If you cannot leave the components in the former, jam them into a corner and use batons to hold them in shape.

The sharper bends of roof-poles, or small bentwood crowns, exert great pressures on the wood fibres, and there is a tendency for the wood to split, or break out, on the outside of the bend. On one inch (25mm) thick roof poles you may lose up to 30 per cent due to break out. To reduce the loss make the roof pole thinner at the bend. With ¾ inch (19mm) thick timber the failure rate is less than 5 per cent. Or use a strap. To bend thicker timbers secure a strap to the outside of the bend. Heavy-duty nylon webbing, which covers the entire width of the timber, should be clamped tightly in place before bending. The use of a spring-steel strap is even more effective (fig 67).

Bending crowns of less than 30 inches (75cm) in diameter is virtually impossible without a strap. A three-foot crown will bend without a strap only if it is perfectly straight grained and knot free. Larger crowns present less of a problem.

CHAPTER 8

Building a Mongolian *ger*

Eighteen foot Mongolian *ger*. Made from English ash by Woodland Yurts

The wall

The typical Mongolian *ger* has a wall five feet (1.5m) high, consisting of at least four *khana* sections. The typical *khana* has 15 heads. The usual nomad family *ger* has five or six *khana*, with diameters of 18 and 21 feet (5.5m and 6.5m) respectively.

The wall rods (*khar mod*) are between 76 and 88 inches (1.93-2.24m) long with holes spaced seven inches (18cm) apart. Each *khar mod* has either: a single bend, starting about two thirds of the way up the rod, or a double bend, with the top three or four inches (75-100mm) brought back into line with the bottom. This gives the Mongol *ger* wall its distinctive slight taper towards the top.

The seven inch (18cm) hole spacing of the Mongol *ger* provides support for a felt cover, which has less tensile strength than canvas. Using this spacing for a *ger* with a canvas cover will make it unnecessarily cumbersome. A nine inch (23cm) spacing will provide more than enough support but produce a lighter and more manageable frame, whilst retaining an authentic look. Increasing the spacing further, to twelve inches (30cm) will reduce the timber requirements and labour greatly and still produce a strong enough, yet lightweight *ger*. The Mongolian *ger* plans in this book use a nine inch (23cm) spacing.

Bending the wall poles

Although not essential, bending the wall rods gives the Mongolian *ger* its distinctive profile, with straight sides, perhaps tapering in slightly towards the shoulder. The work involved is, in fact, not that great; the fixtures will take an hour or so to set up and then the wood can be left to steam. A few minutes each half-hour to remove the poles and push them onto the former is all the work that is required.

The former to produce a simple single bend consists of three round poles 1¼ inches (30mm) in diameter and four or five feet (1.2-1.5m) long. Hammer them into the ground, 22 inches (56cm) apart. Make sure they are in a straight line (*fig 36*).

Fig. 36: The hot wall poles are forced between three upright posts

Once the rods have been steamed, take them out one at a time and force them between these uprights. The middle upright should coincide with a point about three inches (75mm) above the mid-point of the wall rod. To avoid distorting the former, face the wall rods in alternate directions as you stack them up. Leave the rods in the former overnight. The next morning they will have taken on a permanent bend.

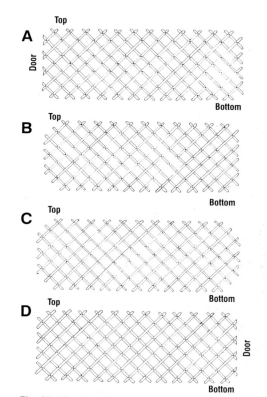

Fig. 37: The four *khana* sections which make the wall of a 16 foot *ger*

Steamed wall poles setting on the former

The door frame *nars*

If you are using round wood follow the instructions given in Chapter Seven. If using sawn timber you will need the following pieces, which should have been planed smooth.

1¼ x 1¼ inches (30 x 30mm) x height of door	2 pieces
2½ x 2 inches (65 x 50mm) x width of door plus 6 inches (15cm)	2 pieces
1½ x ¼ inches (38 x 6mm) x height of door minus 2 inches (50mm)	2 pieces

Make 1¼ x1¼ inch (30x30mm) mortises 1½ inches (32.5mm) deep in the appropriate places on the door top and bottom. The door posts should be a tight fit in these holes. Assemble the frame and glue and nail (use brass nails, iron ones will stain the canvas cover) the two thin batons onto the uprights (*fig 34*).

The crown *tono*

The *tono*, crown, or roof wheel, is probably the most difficult part of the yurt to make. It consists of a wooden 'wheel', between 18 inches and five feet (45-150cm) in diameter, with a raised centre supported by eight spokes. The rim has a number of holes drilled in the outside edge to take the roof poles. Traditionally the finished crown is elaborately decorated to form the major feature of the inside of the yurt. Hardwoods such as beech,

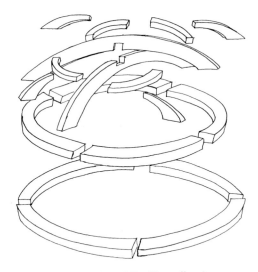

Fig 38: Exploded view of the Mongolian *tono* showing the component parts

oak, or maple make the best *tono*, but softwoods can be used if these are not available (*fig 38*).

The main body of the crown is made in sections. If using one inch (25mm) timber you will need 12 sections. With one and a half inch (38mm) timber eight sections are sufficient. To make these sections you will need a template:

Draw two circles corresponding to the inner and outer rims of the crown on a piece of hardboard or thick card. For a large circle use a piece of wood with two nails hammered through it as a compass, scratching the circle with the point of one nail. Divide this circle exactly into equal quarters. Cut out one of these quarters using a craft knife. Check that this quarter is exactly the same size as the remaining three. If it is, use it as a template for your crown sections (*fig 39*).

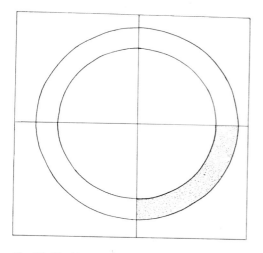

Fig. 39: Marking the template for the *tono* sections

Place the template on the timber and carefully draw around it; a sharp marking knife is more accurate than a pen, and a ball-point pen is more accurate than a pencil. Cut out this shape using an electric jig-saw, or band-saw. Repeat this operation until you have the required number of sections. For more accurate cutting, use a tennon saw for the straight ends.

The sections should now be screwed, glued and clamped together. Lay the sections together. It may be worth swapping them around to get the best fit. Mark where you intend to put the screws. This should be towards the inside edge, so that you do not later hit them and damage the drill when you are making the holes in the outer edge. Drill and countersink screw-holes in the top layer.

Build up the crown a few sections at a time. Lay all of the sections together again. Apply PVA wood glue to the mating faces of three sections, screw them together and clamp the joints using as many clamps as you can. Allow the glue enough time to set before removing the clamps. Repeat this procedure until the circle is complete.

When the glue has set fully, tidy the outer and inner rims with a plane, spokeshave, surform, electric sander, or planer. Any of these tools will do the job adequately. I use an electric planer on the outer rim and a coarse metal sanding disk on the inner. I then finish the job inside and out with a medium sanding disk.

Crown mortises

Mark the outer rim of the crown with equally spaced points, just below the middle of its width, one point for each *uni*. Using an electric drill or a bit and brace, drill a one inch (25mm) hole at each point. These holes should point upwards into the crown at about 25-35°.

To determine the exact angle to drill: find a clear wall. Place the bottom of a roof pole next to the wall and a distance equal to the yurt's radius from the corner. Put a brick or similar weight behind it to stop it slipping back. Lift the top end of the roof pole until it is the equivalent of the crown's radius from the corner, when measured horizontally (use a level). Measure the angle between the pole and the level. This is the angle for the crown

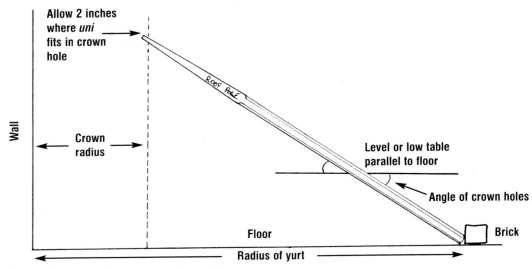

Fig 40: Working out the crown mortise angle

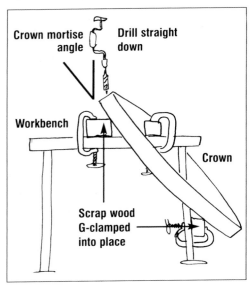

Fig. 41: Using a portable workbench as a jig to drill angled crown holes

mortises (*fig 40*). If you do not have a convenient wall, mark a large right angle on the floor, using string.

To achieve the correct angle, use a portable workbench or a shaving horse with cross pieces clamped in place to hold the *tono* at the required angle from the vertical. Drill straight down, into the edge of the (angled) crown (*fig 41*).

If you want square mortises use a chisel and mallet to knock out the corners of the round hole. Make sure the underside of the hole is supported hard against a wooden block.

The raised crown centre

The traditional Mongolian *tono* centre is made from ten individual components, which are screwed together. Draw the components on cardboard, making sure all ends are square. Cut the patterns out and use

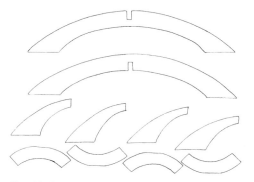

Fig. 42: Component parts of the raised *tono* centre

them as templates. Use the same wood as for the crown wheel, but just a single thickness (*fig 42*).

When you have cut out the sections, chamfer the edges slightly using sandpaper or a chisel. Drill screw-holes, and countersink, all pieces ready for assembly.

The two long pieces should be joined by cutting a slot, the same width as the timber and to half of the depth in the top of one piece. Cut a corresponding groove in the bottom of the other. These pieces should now interlock to form a cross, which you can glue and screw to the top of the crown wheel. Now screw and glue the four inner circle quadrants to the cross–pieces. Then fit the four smaller spokes. The finished *tono* should be painted or given a couple of coats of yacht varnish.

Roof poles *uni*

If using roundwood poles, simply whittle the top three inches to fit into the round holes in the rim of the crown. The fit should not be too tight or the *uni* will become stuck. Nor should they be too loose, or the crown will be unstable. Use a sharp knife or surform tool to round the sharp edges of the bottom ends.

If you are using square section timber, the top ends need to be tapered to fit into the crown mortises, whilst the main shaft needs to be rounded. This shaping can be easily achieved using an electric planer. If an electric planer is not available, good results can be achieved using a draw knife, but this requires a lot more work.

Start by rounding the shafts. An attractive octagonal finish can be achieved by simply chamfering the corners to the maximum depth (for most planers) from the bottom of the pole to 30 inches (75cm) from the top.

Make a simple fixture by nailing two parallel batons, one inch apart to the bench. Clamp a lump of wood to the top end of the bench and another to one of the batons to stop the plane 30 inches (75cm) from the top.

The pole will sit diagonally between the batons; push the pole top against the end stop and plane off the top corner. The second block will stop the machine at the correct point. Most planers have a groove in the foot plate for this type of work. If you want a (nearly) perfectly round shaft, chamfer off the eight new corners, but take a much shallower cut (*fig 43*).

Fig. 43: The chamfered *uni* shaft

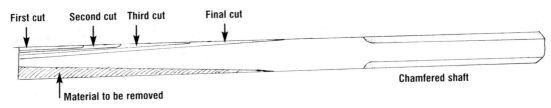

First cut | Second cut | Third cut | Final cut

Chamfered shaft

Material to be removed

Fig. 44: Using an electric planer to taper the *uni* tops

To taper the top part of the *uni*, make a gauge by cutting a square hole the same size as a crown mortise in a piece of wood. Push the tapered ends into this hole to check the fit.

Now sit the *uni* flat on the bench, and set your planer to take a cut of about ⅟₁₆ inch (1.5mm). Make the first cut from about four inches (100mm) back to the end (run the plane off of the end). Now make another cut starting eight inches (20cm) from the end, followed by another 12 inches (30cm), and another 20 inches (50cm) back (*fig 44*). Plane the remaining three edges in this way. Check the taper by pushing it into the guage hole, it should go in two or three inches (50-75mm); if necessary adjust the depth of cut or the number of cuts to give exactly the right taper.

Use sandpaper to remove any sharp or rough edges, drill two holes at the bottom end. Generally one hole ¾ inches (20mm) and 1½ inches (32mm) from the end, but hold it up to your *khana* for a more accurate measure. These holes should be at 45° to the flats of the tapered top. Round the bottom end with a surform tool (*fig 45*).

Four *uni* need not be drilled as they attach to the top of the door. These four poles traditionally sit in shaped recesses in the door lintel. A simpler and equally effective method is to use wooden or brass pegs in the *uni*, which fit in holes in the lintel. The four *uni* need to be cut a few inches shorter than the rest, to allow for the straight door top. The only practical way to know how much to cut off is to put up the yurt.

Put up the yurt frame, leaving four free holes in the *tono* facing the door. Push the tops of the *uni* into the *tono* and leave the bottom ends resting on top of the lintel. Mark where they will need to be cut. The end should be cut at an angle so that it sits flat against the top of the lintel. When you have cut the ends off, put them back in place and drill down through the *uni* and lintel. Start with a small pilot hole. Drill the final hole in the *uni* to take a ⅟₁₆ inch (8mm) (or similar) dowel, which should be a tight fit. Glue the dowel in place with at least an inch (25cm) projecting. Drill the hole in the lintel slightly bigger, so that the dowel fits loosely into it.

Fig. 45: The finished bottom end of the *uni*

Simple *bagana*, made using extra *tono* sections. Supporting beech *tono* of hazel *ger*

Roof pole securing loops *sagaldarga*

Each roof pole is secured to the top of the *khana* by a simple string loop or *sagaldarga* (meaning *bridle* in Mongolian). The loop should be on the lower right hand side of the pole, as it will be seen from inside the yurt. Use a spare offcut of a wall pole as a gauge and, decide which side the loop needs to be on. Knot the string at one end and push the other through one hole, around the gauge piece and back through the other hole, pull it tight and knot the free end.

Bagana

Simple and attractive *bagana* tops can be made using two extra *tono* rim sections, and four of the small *tono* spokes. If you are planning on fitting *bagana* cut these extra pieces out when you are making the *tono*. Make the posts from 2 x 2 inch (50 x 50mm) timber. Make the *bagana* last of all. Put up the frame and measure the exact height from the ground to the bottom of the *tono*. Cut the posts to this height, minus the thickness of the top piece. Screw and glue the top in place. Screw one of the small spokes as a bracket on either side of the post under the top.

Assembling the frame

1. Choose a suitable piece of ground, as flat as possible – but don't worry if it slopes. If you have a wooden or concrete floor it is a good idea to draw a circle on the ground using a marker pen, crayon or chalk; use a piece of string and a nail to form a compass. Make the circle exactly the diameter of the *ger*.

2. Open the *khana* sections and spread them into an approximate circle. The top half of the *khana* bends in towards the centre. The top has the guide string (if fitted) close to it and shorter pole ends. Open as wide as the guide string allows. The ends cut at 45° attach to the door frame; leave a gap here. The other ends should interlock (*see p 37*).

3. Lash the *khana* sections together using rope or webbing tapes.

4. Tie the door frame to the open ends of the *khana*. The thin batons attached to the uprights go on the outside. The wall ends sit tight against the frame and behind the batons.

5. Adjust the walls to form an exact circle. Either use a pre-marked circle as a guide or use roof poles to gauge the circle. The roof poles are usually exactly half the diameter. On smaller *gers* hold two poles end-to-end to check the diameter in several places. On larger *gers* place eight poles on the ground with their ends just meeting in the middle and radiating out to the wall; adjust the wall to line

up with the outside ends. **It is important to get the circle exact, at least ± 1 inch (25mm).**

6. Tie the tension rope around the entire yurt. Tie it securely to each door post, near the top, pull it tight enough that it will not slip down or sag, but not so tight that it distorts the circle. It helps if you pass it through (between, not inside) three or four of the Vs (crossovers) at the top of the wall poles, this will stop it falling down. **Do not attempt to fit the roof without the tension rope in place.** Without this rope the roof will force the wall outwards and may damage it.

7. Attach the roof poles to the *khana* heads. The loop fits over the inner wall pole with the *bogs* (roof pole end) sitting in the V(*fig 32*).

8. On *gers* up to 14 feet (4.25m) in diameter the roof can be raised by one person, on larger *gers* two people are needed. Select four roof poles at 90° to each other. Hold the crown above your head, you may need to stand on a box to reach high enough, or use the *bagana*, if you have any. Insert the four roof poles into the corresponding holes in the crown (easier with a friend to help). Insert a further four roof poles, these should now support the crown. Lie on the floor in the middle of the yurt and look up. Check that the poles enter the crown at an angle of 90°. If they do not move them to the holes where they do.

9. Fit the remaining roof poles. The four poles with pegs in place of strings fit between the crown and the door (*fig 34*).

10. Pull the crown down hard to seat the roof poles. Stand back and check that the crown is level. If not, pull down hard on the high side. If you cannot get the crown to sit level, it is because the yurt is not circular. Picking up the

entire frame, and putting it down again will usually fix this.

11. Tie the end of the canvas tension band to the frame, inside of the door. Pass it around the outside of the yurt, where the roof and walls meet. Pull it tight as you go. Tie the other end securely to the frame inside of the door.

12. You are now ready to fit the cover (*see p 115*).

Timber floor

If the yurt is to be used as a semi-permanent dwelling a timber floor, raised three inches off the ground on bearers of treated 3x3 inches (75x75mm) timber will improve comfort greatly. Make the floor at least six inches (15cm) wider than the yurt. Use tongue and grooved pine, reclaimed floorboards, plywood or chipboard. By drilling holes in the floor in front of the stove, air to feed the fire is drawn under the yurt, rather than through any gaps, reducing draughts and further improving comfort.

The traditional Mongolian floor is made from planks with a metal, concrete or stone hearth in the centre. It dismantles into nine pieces for transport (*fig. 23*). Modern American yurts use timber floors consisting of radial segments, which join to form a circle.

CHAPTER 9

The cover

Tools

It is a common misconception that you need an industrial sewing machine to make a yurt cover. In an ideal world an industrial machine is preferable, one with a walking foot or needle feed is even better. However, a perfectly good cover can be made using an ordinary domestic machine.

Luckily, the best domestic machines are also the cheapest and easiest to find. The old black Singer or Jones machines are ideal. Avoid modern machines with a lot of fancy stitches. An electric machine is quick, but a hand machine is easy to use and not too slow. It is easy to convert one sort to the other. Treadle machines are difficult to use whilst simultaneously struggling with the heavy cover. A suitable machine can be found for £10 or less at most auctions or car boot sales.

Materials
■ Needles and thread

If you have an industrial machine, use M25 polyester/cotton thread, and 19 gauge needles. For a domestic machine, use M36 polyester/cotton thread, with a 16 gauge needle. If M36 poly/cotton thread is unavailable, use the strongest you can find. If you can break it with your fingers it is probably not strong enough. You will need several hundred metres of thread, and a few spare needles.

■ Canvas

Cotton canvas is best. The material should be at least waterproofed. Fire and rot proofing increases safety and longevity. Canvas is waterproof and breathable, so there are no problems with condensation and a fly-sheet is unnecessary. Its weight provides extra stability.

Twelve ounce canvas is heavy enough while still being easy to sew on a domestic machine. Ten ounce is easy to work, but a bit flimsy so it may flap in the wind. Fifteen ounce canvas gives a good heavy cover, but is hard to sew and takes a long time to dry out once wet.

The waterproof skirt is made from PVC-coated fabric, which is almost indestructible. This material makes an extremely durable groundsheet.

Basic technique

Each yurt frame is unique in size and shape so it is not possible to make the complete cover to a pre-made pattern. A cover blank can be made using the worked examples in this book, providing the yurt diameter, *uni* length and crown diameter are exactly as specified. However, it is always better to fit the whole cover to the assembled frame. The final fitting will need the assembled frame.

When the frame is finished put it up in the garden (when there is little risk of rain) and make the cover to fit it, or fit the cover

blank. It will take about three working days to make the complete cover.

The canvas will shrink slightly (about 2-5 per cent in length) when it first gets wet so allow an overlap of at least eight inches (20cm) between the roof and walls and make the walls at least three feet longer than the circumference of the frame (minus door). Alternatively pre-shrink the canvas.

Joining canvas

There are three techniques for sewing the canvas together, depending on the nature of the edges. The raw canvas comes with a selvedge, where there are no loose fibres to fray. Once the canvas has been cut the new edge has loose fibres which will fray if left exposed. So, any cut edges must not be exposed. It is worth practising these techniques on some scrap material before setting to work on the actual cover. Making the tension band first allows one to become familiar with the machine and material before tackling the main cover.

Selvedge to selvedge

The two edges are overlapped by about an inch (25mm) and sewn with a double row of stitches. There is a coloured thread along the edge of most canvas to help line the two sheets up.

Selvedge to cut edge

1. Place the cut sheet on top of the uncut one. The cut edge should be about ¾ inch (18mm) back from the lower selvedge. Sew the sheets together with a line of stitches ¼ inch (6mm) from the cut edge.

2. Now turn both sheets over and pull them in opposite directions. Sew through both sheets following the selvedge (*fig 46*).

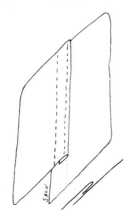

Fig. 46: Joining canvas, selvedge to cut edge

Cut edge to cut edge

This is a common sewing technique called the French seam. Both cut edges are hidden.

1. Place one cut sheet on top of the other. The top cut edge should be about ¾ inch (18mm) back from the lower one. Sew the sheets together with a line of stitches ¼ inch (6mm) back from the cut edge of the top sheet.

2. Now turn both sheets over and pull them in opposite directions. Tuck the cut edge

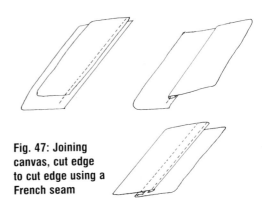

Fig. 47: Joining canvas, cut edge to cut edge using a French seam

under as you sew it down with the second seam (*fig 47*).

Making the cover

The cover is made in four sections:

The roof

There are two methods for making the roof cover: overlapping sheets, or interlocking triangles. The overlapping sheet technique requires less cutting and produces more waterproof joints. However, it produces a slightly less attractive cover and involves manipulating larger canvas sheets through the machine. In Mongolia this method is used to make heavy-duty waterproof canvas outer covers.

The interlocking triangle technique produces a cover, attractive from inside the yurt as few or no seams are visible. More cutting of canvas and sewing is required, but shorter seams and smaller sheet sizes make sewing easier. The seams radiate from the centre, so water runs down them, creating a (theoretical) potential for leakage. The larger number of seams also increases the potential for leakage. However, in practice these covers rarely leak. For the bentwood yurt this is the only practical method to get a good fit. In Mongolia this method is used to make decorative lightweight cotton covers. Before you start work on the roof make sure you have plenty of space, thread, spare needles, good-quality dressmaking pins, a pencil, tape measure, and a pair of scissors. Put up the yurt frame and set up your sewing machine in a large space close by.

Overlapping sheet method

This technique can be used for any size *ger* for which you have no pattern (*fig 48*).

1. Cut sheets A, B and C to length (note angled ends to B and C): Length of sheet A = Length of *uni* x 2 + distance over top of *tono* + 30 inches (76mm) Length of short edge of sheets B and C = (½ length of sheet A) - (¼ inner diameter of *tono*)

2. Sew sheets A, B and C together as illustrated. Use a one inch (2.5cm) overlap and a double seam. Sheets B and C should overlap sheet A to allow water run-off.

3. Place sheet A, B, and C on the frame and pull the two overlapping ends of B and C together so that sheet A sits neatly on the frame with no creases or sags and an equal overlap at either side. Pin sheets B and C together using a straight line of pins from the overlap angle (angle X) to the central hole.

4. Measure angle X, and the length needed for sheets D and E. Make a small mark at the front and back edges so that you can identify the underside after the cover is removed.

5. Take the cover off and sew sheets E and D in place. Make sure they join the underside of sheets A, B and C.

6. Refit the cover and measure how long sheets F and G need to be. Mark the underside of the edges of sheets D and E.

7. Take the cover off and sew sheets F and G into place.

This is the complete cover blank for a ten or twelve foot *ger*. For larger *gers* add more sheets.

When the cover blank is completed fit it over the frame. Mark the position of the crown opening. Cut out this opening and sew strong webbing around the inner edge of the circle.

Refit the cover blank and cut away excess canvas to give a hem at least ten inches (more if possible) below the shoulder. Make a suitable cut out for the entrance. Pin darts at regular intervals around the sides to bring them parallel with the wall. Cut around the

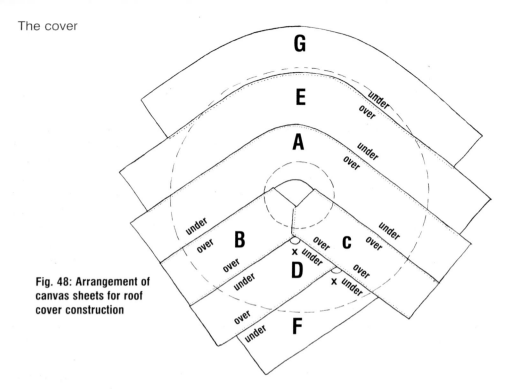

Fig. 48: Arrangement of canvas sheets for roof cover construction

bottom edge again. Measure down from the shoulder starting at the highest point to give a straight hem. Sew a 1½ inch (38mm) hem around the bottom and fit a pair of brass grommets six inches (15cm) apart every two feet (60cm) (figs 85 & 86).

Sew at least four canvas triangles fitted with grommets into the hem at regular intervals for guy-rope attachment.

The wall

The wall cover has just three important dimensions: length, width (height) and skirt length. The length of the wall must be about ten per cent longer than is needed to stretch

around the yurt from door-post to door-post. This allows for shrinkage when the canvas gets wet, and for slight variations in diameter, which may occur each time the yurt is put up.

The wall height should be at least four inches (100mm) less than the *khana* height, so that the bottom of the canvas is not constantly in contact with wet grass or mud. The gap at the bottom is filled with the plastic skirt. The canvas is supplied in rolls 36 inches (91cm) wide; for walls up to 44 inches (112cm) high use a single width plus the skirt to provide sufficient height. For a four-foot (120cm) wall use one and a quarter widths of canvas plus the skirt. For a four foot six inch (135cm) wall use one and a third widths plus the skirt. For a five foot (150cm) wall use one and a half widths plus the skirt.

The skirt length should be the exact distance from door-post to door-post around the yurt, for a perfect fit. I always make my skirts 12 inches (30cm) shorter. Making the skirt slightly shorter is a convenient way to ensure some ventilation when the door and örkh are closed; this is particularly important if you have a fire or gas appliance burning inside. The skirt should be long enough to tuck under the khana feet. If you have a groundsheet, which fits under the feet and up the outside of the khana, the skirt need only reach to the ground.

Put up the yurt frame and measure the height and the circumference of the walls, excluding the door, or calculate the circumference. Be sure to allow for the thickness of the khana, which can make the outside circumference up to 12 inches (30cm) greater than the inside. The top sheet should overlap on the outside of the bottom one by about an inch (25mm) so that rain runs off easily. Make a good 1½

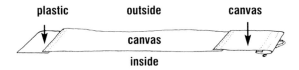

Fig. 49: Section of wall cover with hanging loops at the top and plastic skirt at the bottom

inch (38mm) hem at the top and at each end (*fig 49*).

The walls hang from the *khana* tops. The simplest method of attaching the wall is to fit brass grommets into the top and end hems of the wall. These are spaced equal to the distance between two crossovers at the top of the *khana*. Tie a short string loop through each of the top grommets. Each loop will fit loosely over the top of one wall pole.

A better system, particularly on larger *gers*, uses a continuous string with free loops every few inches: Sew a piece of nylon cord around the inside of the top hem, leave free loops, six inches (15cm) long and three inches (75mm) high every four inches (100mm). Tie a three foot (1m) length of string to each of the end grommets (*fig 50*).

Long walls can be difficult to handle, especially to fold neatly. If the yurt is more than 12 feet (3.6m) in diameter it is worth making the wall in two halves. Work out the length for a one-piece wall, divide it by two and add nine inches (22.5cm). Make the two halves as for a single wall, with the addition of a six inch (15cm) hem at the back. The skirt should go right to the back end of each section. On one section sew a length of nylon cord down the middle of the back hem. Leave four inch (10cm) loops in this cord every four inches, and about two feet (60cm) over at the bottom. Insert a line of grommets on the wide hem of the other half. These grommets should be in the middle of the hem, every four inches

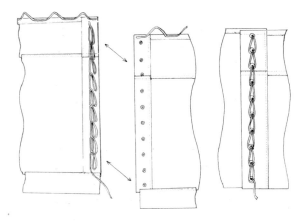

Fig. 50: Using nylon cord and grommets to lace two wall halves together

(100mm), to correspond with the position of the loops. The two halves can now be put in place one at a time and laced together at the back. Use Velcro as well as lacing to give a more weatherproof join (*fig 50*).

The crown cover *örkh*

Make a four pointed canvas star, by sewing triangular corners to a square centrepiece. The centre must be large enough to cover the crown and overlap the hole by at least six inches (15cm). Put one or two darts in the central square to give a convex profile to fit over the raised crown middle. Attach eight foot (2.4m) lengths of rope to each point. It is easy to sew four triangular, or two semi-circular clear plastic windows into this cover if desired (*fig 51*).

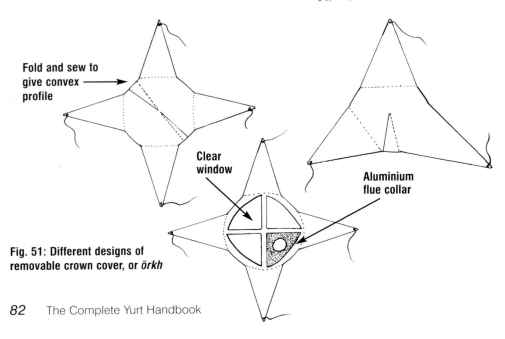

Fold and sew to give convex profile

Clear window

Aluminium flue collar

Fig. 51: Different designs of removable crown cover, or *örkh*

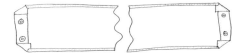

Fig. 52: The tension band; a long strip of canvas which holds the roof poles in place and stops the weight of the roof pushing the walls outwards

The tension band

This band, which passes around the top of the *khana* and the ends of the roof poles has three functions: To hold the *uni* in place, to protect the roof cover from abrasion, and as an additional safeguard against the weight of the roof pushing the walls outwards.

Take a piece of canvas as long as the wall and nine inches (23cm) wide. Sew a strong hem along either side of its length and a 1½ inch (38mm) hem at each end.

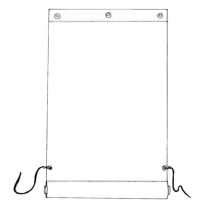

Fig. 53: A simple canvas door, which hangs from hooks on the lintel. The bottom is weighted with a piece of wood in the hem

On very large yurts reinforce the band by sewing strong nylon cord inside the hems. Fit two brass grommets at either end, one in each corner. At each end tie a three foot (1m) length of rope (*fig 52*).

Canvas door

A simple curtain door can be fashioned from a length of canvas with a good three inch (75mm) hem at the top and bottom. Grommets are fitted into the top hem, so that the door can hang from hooks in the lintel. The bottom of the door can be weighted by sliding a piece of wood through the bottom hem. Grommets can be fitted in the edge, near the bottom to tie the door shut (*fig 53*).

Windows

Windows can be sewn into the wall or crown cover. A wall-fitted window is easy to make separately. It can then be sewn into an appropriately sized hole cut in the canvas. Make the clear plastic window with a two inch (50mm) frame and reinforce it with canvas or webbing sewn horizontally and vertically every six inches (15cm). A canvas blind, which can be held open with tapes, and shut with Velcro, is a simple and useful addition. (*See p 86*).

Insulation

Thick felt is the traditional insulating material. Wool carpet underlay is the nearest thing that is easily available in the UK. This has the advantage of being flame

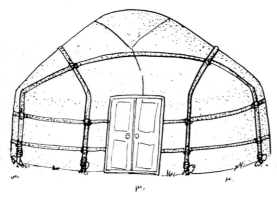

Fig. 54: Extra ropes to secure the yurt in high winds

retardant, but tends to shed hair more readily than real felt. Blankets, horticultural fleece, or carpet can also be used. The insulation is sandwiched between the frame and cover. The insulation is held firmly in place and need only be cut roughly to size.

Extreme weatherproofing

For summer use the *ger* will stand up to most weather without being anchored to the ground. However, it is advisable to use at least four pegs and guy ropes to hold the roof cover down. These are pulled straight down to the ground. There is no need to pull them out from the body of the yurt as with a normal tent.

On an exposed site or in preparation for winter gales, three foot (1m) wooden stakes should be driven into the ground inside the yurt near the door and at the *khana* junction. The frame can be securely tied to these stakes. To secure the cover, four ropes 25 feet (7.5m) long should be tied together to form a six to nine foot (2-3m) square at their middle. This can be thrown over the yurt and pegged down tightly at eight points (*fig 54*).

If the *ger* is likely to have to bear the weight of a thick snow covering a pair of *bagana* should be fitted to support the crown. These are traditionally brightly painted and always kept in place.

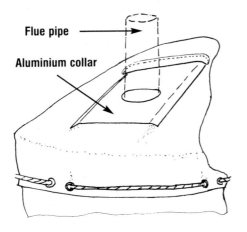

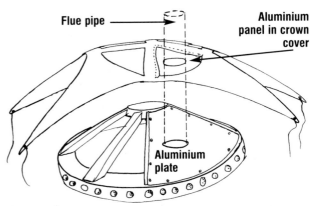

Fig. 55: Central and side-mounted aluminium flue collars

Fire

A fire or stove is a pleasant luxury during the summer and a necessity for winter use. However, as with any tent, it is potentially very dangerous to light a fire in the yurt. Do so at your own risk. A few precautions and modifications can reduce this risk. The fire or stove is traditionally placed in the centre of the yurt directly below the crown. In a small yurt this location might prove too intrusive so a stove can be placed towards the side.

A traditional open fire with smoke leaving through the crown seems like a pleasant idea, but the yurt rapidly fills with thick smoke and so this is completely impractical. This problem can be reduced slightly by using a very large open crown, and/or a tall, steep roof to draw the smoke out. A raised top to the centre was traditionally used in Mongolia to draw the smoke out, but I have never seen this in use, so cannot comment upon its efficacy. Using charcoal rather than wood reduces smoke, but make sure there is plenty of ventilation. A flue pipe with an inverted funnel at its base, supported just above an open fire should draw smoke out.

A metal woodburning stove is a much more practical solution. The smallest stove will provide more than enough heat. Both the stove and the flue-pipe will become extremely hot during use and any combustible material (wood or canvas) in contact with these will catch fire. Wood or canvas within a few inches

of the stove or flue-pipe will rapidly char.

To reduce any fire risk it is necessary to keep the flue-pipe separated from the frame and cover. This is achieved by making a collar of 1mm aluminium sheet. For a central stove, remove one of the eight crown spokes and fill the gap with a piece of aluminium with a hole cut in it to take the flue-pipe (*fig 55*).

A similar aluminium sheet must be sewn or joined with Velcro to the crown cover. The use of Velcro allows the aluminium to be replaced with waterproof canvas or plastic if the stove is not in place. For a side-mounted stove leave a space of at least 18 inches (45cm) between the stove and the wall. Remove one of the roof poles above the stove to leave a gap, cut a hole in the canvas in this space. Cut out an 18 inch (45cm) square of aluminium sheet with a round hole in the centre to take the flue-pipe. Smooth the edges and corners and bend the sides down slightly with the fold two inches (50mm) from the edge. Use Velcro to join this sheet to the canvas, make a flap in the cover to overlap the top of the plate and allow water to run off.

CHAPTER 10

Worked examples

The following examples have been tried and tested. They are popular sizes, one of them should be suitable for most uses. The hole spacing is nine inches (23cm). This will give a very robust yurt with an authentic look. A lighter version can be made by increasing the hole spacing to 12 inches (30cm). The lightweight *ger* is less strong, but still very robust and requires a lot less wood in its construction. To make a lightweight *ger* refer to the bentwood yurt examples *(see page 94)* for quantities of timber, number and spacing of holes etc.

Ten foot *ger*
An ideal size for family camping or a small communal area. Will fit in all but the very smallest car. Insulate with felt or carpet underlay and fit a stove for a great sauna.

Yurt diameter	10' (3m)
Wall height	4' (1.3m)
Roof height	6'9" (2.05m)
Number of *khana*	2
Door height	52" (1.32m)
Door width (internal)	34" (86cm)
***Tono* diameter**	24" (60cm)
***Tono* holes** (number and angle)	34 holes 34º
***Uni* length**	62" (1.57m)
Number of *uni*	34 (30 to *khana*, 4 to door)
***Khana* rod length**	60" (1.52m)
Hole spacing	9" (23cm)
Holes per rod	7
Total wall rods (including rods to be cut to make ends)	68 (52 full rods +16 for ends)
End pieces (angled)*	7 up (2), 7 down (2), 5 up (2), 5 down (2), 3 up (2), 3 down (2)
End Pieces (square)**	6 up (2), 6 down (2), 5 up (1), 5 down (1), 4 up (1) 4 down (1), 3 up (1), 3 down (1), 2 up (1), 2 down (1)

End pieces

Lengths of end pieces are given as the number of holes, or un-drilled crossover points, from the top, or bottom. So, for six up, start at the bottom and count six holes/crossover points. Cut the rod above the sixth hole or crossover point.

★ Cut angled end pieces at 45°, with the middle of the cut 2 inches (50mm) above last hole/crossover. Angled pieces come in pairs, one for either side of the door. Therefore, one should be cut in one direction and one in the other.

★★ Square end pieces are cut 3½ inches (90mm) past the last hole/crossover.

Twelve foot *ger*

Higher walls and extra floor space make this an ideal holiday home, studio, small shop, or display area. Will fit in an average-sized car. There is room for a central wood-buring stove. Placing the stove near the wall (not closer than 18" [45cm]) gives more free space.

Yurt diameter	12' (3.65m)
Wall height	5' (1.52m)
Roof height	8'6" (2.6m)
Number of *khana*	3
Door height	64" (1.63m)
Door width (internal)	34" (86cm)
***Tono* diameter**	30" (75cm)
***Tono* holes** (number and angle)	39 holes 36°
***Uni* length**	72" (1.82m)
Number of *uni*	39 (35 to khana, 4 to door)
***Khana* rod length**	78" (1.98m)
Hole spacing	9" (23cm)
Holes per rod	9 (7 holes, 2 spaces) [see fig 31]
Total wall rods (including rods to be cut to make ends)	85 (50 full rods +35 for ends)
End pieces (angled)*	8 up (2), 8 down (2), 6 up (2), 6 down (2), 4 up (2), 4 down (2), 2 up (2), 2 down(2)
End pieces (square)**	8 up (4), 8 down (4), 7 up (2), 7 down (2), 6 up (2), 6 down (2), 5 up (2), 5 down (2), 4 up (2), 4 down (2), 3 up (2), 3 down (2), 2 up (2), 2 down (2)

Sixteen foot *ger*

A huge space, big enough for a permanent dwelling, classroom, workshop, café, or restaurant. Can be carried in a medium-sized car, with the *uni* on the roof rack.

Yurt diameter	16' (4.88m)
Wall height	5' (1.52m)
Roof height	9' (2.73m)
Number of *khana*	4
Door height	64" (1.63m)
Door width (internal)	36" (91cm)
***Tono* diameter**	34" (86cm)
***Tono* holes** (number and angle)	52 holes 33º
***Uni* length**	8' (2.44m)
Number of *uni*	52 (48 to khana, 4 to door)
***Khana* rod length**	78" (1.98m)
Hole spacing	9" (23cm)
Holes per rod	9 (7 holes, 2 spaces) [*fig 31*]
Total wall rods (including rods to be cut to make ends)	110 (64 full rods +46 for ends)
End pieces (angled)*	8 up (2), 8 down (2), 6 up (2), 6 down (2), 4 up (2), 4 down (2), 2 up (2), 2 down (2)
End pieces (square)**	8 up (6), 8 down (6), 7 up (3), 7 down (3), 6 up (3), 6 down (3), 5 up (3), 5 down (3), 4 up (3), 4 down (3), 3 up (3), 3 down (3), 2 up (3), 2 down (3)

Cover designs for specific yurts

When making a *ger* with a completely new set of dimensions it is necessary to make up the cover, sheet-by-sheet to fit it exactly to the roof. Once the cover has been fitted, make a note of all dimensions. With these dimensions subsequent covers for the same size yurt can be made, following the pattern. The yurt only needs to be put up once, for the final fitting.

The following examples are tried-and-tested patterns for the most popular-size yurts. For them to work the frame must follow the specifications for yurt diameter, roof-pole length, and crown diameter excatly.

Stage one shows the uncut sheets, which form the front of the cover. Sew these together, as shown, ensuring that the overlap will allow water to run over, rather than into the join.

For **stage two**: lay these sheets on the ground, or with the centre on a table. Pull the two angled ends, one over the other, until their free edges meet at exactly the required angle. Ensure that the gap between the sheets forms a triangle, with the two cut sides of equal length. Pin the overlapping sheets in a straight line between the apex of the middle triangle and the measured angle.

Cut away excess material on the top sheet, but allow a generous hem of at least two inches from the line of pins. Sew along the line of pins. Now sew a hem where you just cut away the excess. Turn the cover over and cut away the excess on the other side at least two inches (50mm) from the seam. Now sew a hem along this cut edge.

Take a moment to think which way up the cover will go, so that you can attach the angled sheets underneath to allow water run-off. Now attach the angled sheets. Use French seams where necessary to hide and protect the cut edge. The blank cover is now ready for fitting to the frame.

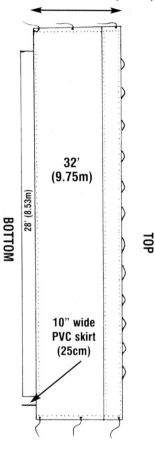

1¼ widths of canvas 43" (109cm)

32' (9.75m)

28' (8.53m)

BOTTOM

TOP

10" wide PVC skirt (25cm)

Fig. 58: The wall of the ten foot *ger*, which hangs from the *khana* heads, wraps around the door posts and is secured to the *khana* at either end

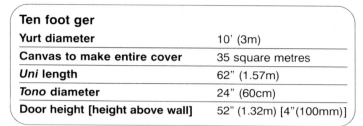

Ten foot ger	
Yurt diameter	10' (3m)
Canvas to make entire cover	35 square metres
***Uni* length**	62" (1.57m)
***Tono* diameter**	24" (60cm)
Door height [height above wall]	52" (1.32m) [4"(100mm)]

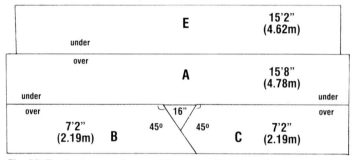

E — 15'2" (4.62m)

under / over

A — 15'8" (4.78m)

under / over

16" / 45° / 45°

B — 7'2" (2.19m) / C — 7'2" (2.19m)

Fig. 56: Ten foot *ger* roof cover: Stage one. The uncut sheets which form the front part of the roof cover

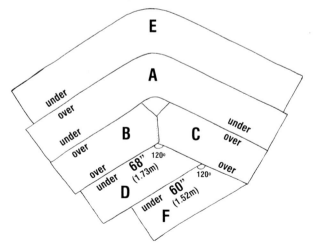

E / A / under over / B / C / under over / over under / 68" (1.73m) 120° / 60" (1.52m) 120° / D / F / under

Fig. 57: Ten foot roof cover: Stage two. The two angled sheets are added to give the conical cover blank, ready for its final fitting to the frame

Twelve foot ger

Yurt diameter	12' (3.65m)
Canvas to make entire cover	50 square metres
Uni length	6' (1.83m)
Tono diameter	30" (76cm)
Door height [height above wall]	64" (1.63m) [4"(100mm)]

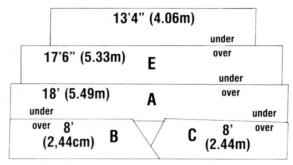

Fig. 59: Twelve foot *ger* roof cover: Stage one

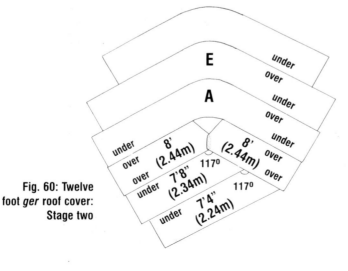

Fig. 60: Twelve foot *ger* roof cover: Stage two

Fig. 61: Twelve foot *ger* wall cover

Sixteen foot ger

Yurt diameter	16' (4.88m)
Canvas to make entire cover	70 square metres
Uni **length**	8' (2.44m)
Tono **diameter**	34" (86cm)
Door height [height above wall]	64" (1.63m) [4"(100mm)]

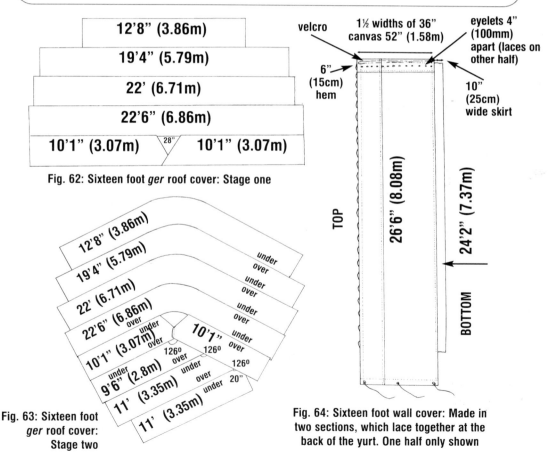

12'8" (3.86m)

19'4" (5.79m)

22' (6.71m)

22'6" (6.86m)

10'1" (3.07m)   28"   **10'1" (3.07m)**

Fig. 62: Sixteen foot *ger* roof cover: Stage one

12'8" (3.86m)

19'4" (5.79m)

22' (6.71m)

22'6" (6.86m) over

10'1" (3.07m) under over

under *10'1"* under over

126° 126° 126°

under *9'6" (2.8m)* over under over 20"

11' (3.35m) under

11' (3.35m)

under over under over under over

Fig. 63: Sixteen foot
ger roof cover:
Stage two

velcro

1½ widths of 36"
canvas 52" (1.58m)

eyelets 4"
(100mm)
apart (laces on
other half)

6"
(15cm)
hem

10"
(25cm)
wide skirt

TOP

26'6" (8.08m)

24'2" (7.37m)

BOTTOM

Fig. 64: Sixteen foot wall cover: Made in
two sections, which lace together at the
back of the yurt. One half only shown

CHAPTER 11

The Bentwood yurt

An English-made bentwood yurt frame in ash by Woodland Yurts

The construction of the bentwood yurts is similar to that of the Mongolian *ger*. The major difference is in the roof construction, which requires steam bending of the poles and crown. There is less need for power tools in the construction of the crown, but a steamer is essential.

The door

The door of the bentwood yurt is identical to that of the Mongolian *ger* described earlier. The addition of an arched lintel gives a bit more headroom to the entrance and complements the overall curved shape.

The roof poles

It is the steam-bent roof poles that give the bentwood yurt its distinctive rounded shape (*fig 65*). The roof poles can be made using straight grained, square (1¼x 1¼ inches [32x32mm]) or rectangular (1½x ¾ inches [38x19mm]) section sawn timber. Or use roundwood poles 1-1½ inches (25-38mm) in diameter. The bottom two feet (60cm) of square-section timber

Fig. 65: A bentwood yurt roof pole

should be flattened to ¾ inch (19mm) thick, either with a plane or drawknife to give an easier to bend rectangular profile.

The fixture

The fixture for bending roof poles needs to be solid. Great force is needed to bend the poles and any part of the fixture that is not secure will be pushed out of the ground.

An effective fixture can be made using a completely empty 15kg Calor-gas cylinder, or some other similar-sized cylinder, which will not be crushed by the pressure of the bending poles. Lay the cylinder on its side and secure it in place with pegs driven into the ground. Drive at least three large pegs firmly into the ground about 15 inches (38cm) in front of the cylinder and at an angle of about 60°. The tops should protrude at least six inches (15cm) and point towards the cylinder. Attach a 3x1 inch (7.5x2.5cm) board to the inside faces of the pegs.

Secure a sturdy bar horizontally, a couple of inches above the ground, three or four feet (1m) behind the cylinder. Use at least eight large pegs and ropes to secure it in position.

To bend the poles place the bottom of the hot steamed rod against board. Carefully, but quickly bend the rod over the cylinder to its final position (bend it a bit extra as it will spring back when removed). Secure it in place using strong cord wrapped around the horizontal bar (*fig 66*).

Bending without a strap

The simplest method of bending is without a strap, but this may result in some breakages. Fibres will split out on the outside of the bend, particularly where the grain of the wood has been cut across. This splitting is known as 'break out'. Minor break out can often be repaired by glueing the fibres back into place. Plane and chamfer sawn timber, or strip the bark from roundwood before steaming.

Place the poles in the steamer for forty minutes, or until they are heated right through. Take them out one at a time and force them

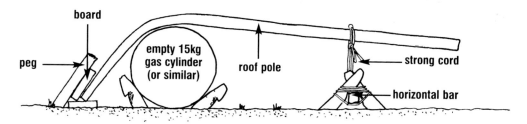

Fig. 66: A simple fixture for bending the roof poles

into the former, before they cool. Ideally, leave them in the former to set for a couple of days.

If you cannot leave the poles on the fixture to set they can be forced into a corner against a wall and held in place with batons for a couple of days. Let them cool on the former before pushing them into a corner.

Bending with a strap

To reduce break out on thicker timbers (1 inch [25mm] or more) use a strap. The theory is that the wood breaks due to the outside of the bend being stretched too far. A strap on the outside limits the stretching, and forces the inside of the bend to compress. Thus the wood is bent with fewer failures. However, this does increase the work involved.

To make the strap use spring steel, or heavy-duty webbing. This must be at least as wide as the wood being bent. Take a four foot (120cm) length and firmly attach a hardwood block to one end. The block should sit around the bottom end of the roof pole.

To use the strap, work fast; fit the wooden block over the bottom of the hot steamed pole. Pull the strap tight against what will be the outside of the curve and clamp the other end securely in place. Push the pole onto the former. Take the strap off once the pole has cooled (fig 67).

When the poles have set take them off the former and cut them exactly to length. Round the bottom with a surform tool and drill a single $\frac{3}{16}$ inch (4.5mm) hole an inch (25mm) from the end.

Make a square section taper to fit the crown mortises on the top of roundwood poles. For sawn timber, cut a tapered tenon to fit into the crown. Use a tenon saw and a chisel. The shoulder of the tenon prevents it from pushing too far through into the centre of the crown.

Use a single piece of string about two feet (60cm) long

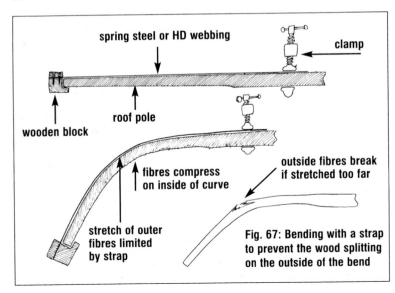

spring steel or HD webbing

clamp

wooden block

roof pole

fibres compress on inside of curve

outside fibres break if stretched too far

stretch of outer fibres limited by strap

Fig. 67: Bending with a strap to prevent the wood splitting on the outside of the bend

threaded through the hole to tie the pole to the *khana* head.

Cut two or three shorter poles to fit to the door lintel. Fit these poles to the lintel using dowels, as described for the Mongolian *ger*.

The walls

Construction of the walls is the same as for the Mongolian *ger*, except the traditional bending of the poles is slightly different. The pole is curved with a single bend from end to end, with its apex in the middle. This is achieved by using three inch (75mm) diameter upright posts for the former. The uprights should be placed so that there is one in the middle and one about four inches (100mm) in from either end of the rods being bent.

The crown

To make a bentwood crown you will need a circular former at least 30 inches (75cm) in diameter. This former needs to be very strong to hold the wood in place without distorting. A suitably sized iron wheel from an old agricultural machine, a section from a large-diameter iron pipe, or an iron cartwheel rim, are all ideal.

Select two pieces of straight-grained, knot-free timber, an inch (25mm) thick and three inches (75mm) wide; sawn timber is fine, but cleft timber is better as fewer of the wood fibres will be broken. Measure the diameter of the former and add two inches (50mm) (to give the final outside diameter of your crown).

Multiply the final diameter by π (3.14) to give the final circumference. Cut the lengths of wood to half of the circumference + twelve inches (30cm). For example: for a 39 inch (1m) wheel, cut the pieces 76½ inches (194cm) long:

$$39 + 2 = 41,$$
$$41 \times \pi = 129,$$
$$\tfrac{1}{2} \times 129 = 64\tfrac{1}{2},$$
$$64\tfrac{1}{2} + 12 = \mathbf{76\tfrac{1}{2}}$$

Finish sawn timber with a plane, or cleft timber with a draw knife. Chamfer the edges. Lay the timber flat and make a mark, square across it, twelve inches (30cm) from one end. Turn the piece over and make another mark 12 inches (30cm) from the other end. Now taper each end on the side of the mark. The taper should start at the mark, becoming thinner towards the end, which should finish at

Fig. 68: One of two sections, which are bent and joined to form the crown rim (*not to scale*)

about ¼ inch (6mm) thick. An electric planer is ideal for making the taper, but a hand plane or a draw knife can be used (*fig 68*).

Steam the two halves for at least 40 minutes, or until they are thoroughly heated. For the next stage you will need an assistant. You must work fast: the wood is hard to bend even when hot, when it cools it is impossible. Have plenty of

G-clamps at the ready. Take one piece out of the steamer. Clamp one end to the former. Force the wood onto the former, working from the clamped end; fit more clamps as you go. Speed is important so do not bother with pieces of wood to stop the clamps marking the crown, it will take too long. Marks can be removed later. If the wood starts to cool and lose flexibility before you have finished, give up and put it back in the steamer. Trying to bend wood that is too cool will result in breakage, or the wood will straighten when taken off of the former.

To bend the second piece: slacken the clamp holding the end with an inside taper. Take the second piece out of the steamer and slide the end with an outside taper under the piece you have just loosened. Clamp it to the former as before. The far end should overlap the other taper, you will need to remove and replace a clamp. Leave the crown clamped in place for a couple of days to set.

Once the wood has set in its new shape the two halves can be joined. Take both halves off the former. They will probably spring out slightly, but don't worry. Apply a liberal coating of wood glue to the mating surfaces of one pair of tapers and clamp them together. Drill two pairs of holes right through each piece near one end of the joint. Each hole of a pair should be at about 45° to the rim, but pointing in opposite directions, as illustrated (*fig 69*). Glue tight-fitting

dowels into the holes. Drill another similar four holes and fit dowels near the other end of the joint. Leave the clamps in place. Now apply glue to the other two tapers and push them together. You may need some help to do this. Clamp the joint firmly. Finish the joint with dowels as before. Traditionally, wet rawhide is bound tightly around the joint, which tightens as it dries, to further strengthen the joint.

Fig. 69: Arrangement of dowels joining the two crown halves

When the glue has fully set, remove the clamps and cut off the protruding ends of the dowels. Remove any clamping marks or other blemishes with sandpaper.

At this point the crown may not be perfectly round. Check the diameter in a couple of places. If it is oval: cut a piece of wood to the desired internal diameter and place it across the narrowest

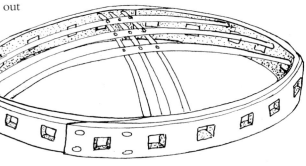

Fig. 70: The complete bentwood crown

part. This will force the crown into a circle. Leave this piece in place until the crown takes on the desired shape. This may take a few weeks, but the crown can still be used in the meantime.

Measure the circumference of the crown, and divide this figure by the number of roof poles, to give the hole spacing. Drill one inch (25mm) holes pointing upwards at an angle of 25-35° (*See Worked Examples or Chapter 8*). Drill right through the crown. To prevent break out where the drill exits put a solid piece of wood firmly against the inner rim. As with the Mongolian *ger*, use a chisel to remove the corners from each hole. Again, put a solid piece of wood inside the crown to reduce break-out (*fig 70*).

Raised centre

The raised centre is easily constructed from slender (½ inch, 12mm) willow or hazel rods, or thin laths. There are various traditional designs. Decide which one you like and make up the centrepiece. Make the rods a few inches longer than the crown diameter. Sit the centrepiece on the crown and bend it up to give the correct height, and determine their finished length. Cut the rods exactly to length. Drill suitably sized holes in the inner rim of the crown close to the top. Push the ends of the rods into the holes. They should stay in place, but glue them if they are loose (*fig 70*).

Assembling the frame

1. Choose a suitable piece of ground, as flat as possible – but don't worry if it slopes.
2. Open the *khana* sections and spread them into an approximate circle. The top half of the *khana* bends in towards the centre. The top has the guide string (if fitted) close to it, and shorter pole ends. Open as wide as the guide string allows. The ends cut at 45° attach to the door frame – leave a gap here. The other ends should interlock.

3. Lash the *khana* sections together using rope or webbing tapes.

4. Tie the door frame to the open ends of the *khana*. The thin battens attached to the uprights go on the outside and the wall ends sit tight against the frame and behind them.

5. Adjust the walls to form an exact circle. On smaller *gers* hold two poles end-to-end to check the diameter in several places. On larger *gers* use a tape measure. **It is important to get the circle exact, at least ± 1 inch (25mm).**

6. Tie the tension rope around the entire yurt. Tie it securely to each door post, near the top. Pull it tight enough that it will not slip down or sag, but not so tight that it distorts the circle. It helps if you pass it through (between, not inside) three or four of the Vs (crossovers) at the top of the wall poles, to stop it falling down. Do not attempt to fit the roof without the tension rope in place. Without this rope the roof will force the walls outwards and may damage them.

7. Tie two roof poles to the *khana* heads. These should be at 120° to each other. Fit the tops into the crown. Push the end

of a third pole into the crown mortise opposite (at 120° to) the other two. Hold the bottom end of this third pole and use it to lift the crown up, into place. Tie the third pole to the appropriate *khana* head.

8. Fit the remaining roof poles.

9. Pull the crown down hard, to seat the roof poles. Stand back and check that the crown is level. If it is not, pull down hard on the high side. If you cannot get the crown to sit level, it is because the yurt is not circular. Picking up the entire frame, and putting it down again will usually fix this.

10. Tie the end of the canvas tension band to the frame, inside of the door. Pass it around the outside of the yurt, where the roof and walls meet. Pull it tight as you go. Tie the other end securely to the frame inside of the door.

11. You are now ready to fit the cover (see p115).

Bentwood yurt covers

Wall, tension band, örkh, door

The wall, tension band, *örkh* and door are made in exactly the same way as for the Mongolian *ger*.

Roof

The roof cover is made from interlocking triangles of canvas. Put up the frame and make a paper pattern of the triangle formed between every third roof pole. The base of the triangle should measure about three feet (91cm). Make the pattern to the outside edge

of both roof poles to give an extra inch or so for the joints. Its base should be about ten inches (25cm) below the ends of the roof poles and its top at least three inches inside the crown. Use the pattern to make an appropriate number of canvas triangles and sew them together. Use French seams where appropriate (*fig 71*).

Place this cover over the frame and mark the central hole. Cut a neat hem around the bottom edge. Take the cover off and sew webbing tape around the central hole. Sew a 1½" hem around the bottom and fit grommets and guy rope attachment points, as for the Mongolian *ger*.

Fig. 71: The roof cover is made from a number of roughly triangular sections sewn together

Bentwood yurts: worked examples

In these examples, I have used a 12 inch (30cm) wall pole spacing to give a lightweight but strong yurt. For a more authentic look and a stronger frame use a nine inch (23cm) spacing. This will require significantly more timber. Refer to the worked examples of Mongolian *gers* for numbers of roof and wall poles. The amount of canvas needed for the cover is about the same as for the Mongol *ger*.

Ten foot yurt	
Yurt diameter	10' (3m)
Wall height	4' (1.3m) (effective wall height 5' [1.5m])
Roof height	7' (2.14m)
Number of *khana*	2
Door height	4'6" (1.37m)
Door width (internal)	34" (86cm)
***Tono* diameter**	30" (75cm)
***Tono* holes**	21
(number and angle)	28°
***Uni* length**	65" (1.65m)
Bend	35°
(angle and distance from bottom)	15" (1.14m)
Number of *uni*	21 (19 to khana, 2 to door)
***Khana* rod length**	66" (1.67m)
Hole spacing	12" (30cm)
Holes per rod	6
Total wall rods (including rods to be cut to make ends)	48 (38 full rods +14 for ends)
End pieces (angled)*	5 down (2), 3 down(2), 6 up (2), 4 up (2), 2 up (2)
End pieces (square)**	5 down (2), 4 down (1), 3 down (1) 2 down (1), 5 up (2), 4 up (1), 3 up (1), 2 up (1)

End pieces

Lengths of end pieces are given as the number of holes from the top, or bottom. So, for six up, start at the bottom and count six holes. Cut the rod above the sixth hole.

★ Cut angled end pieces at 45°, with the middle of the cut 2 inches (50mm) above last hole. Angled pieces come in pairs, one for either side of the door. Therefore, one should be cut in one direction and one in the other.

★★ Square end pieces are cut 3½ inches (90mm) past the last hole.

Twelve foot yurt

Yurt diameter	12' (3.65m)
Wall height	4' (1.3m) (effective wall height 5' [1.5m])
Roof height	8' (2.5m)
Number of *khana*	2
Door height	4'6" (1.37m)
Door width (internal)	34" (86cm)
***Tono* diameter**	41" (1.05m)
***Tono* holes** (number and angle)	28 34º
***Uni* length**	76" (1.93m)
Bend (angle and distance from bottom)	15" (38cm) 35º
Number of *uni*	28 (25 to *khana*, 3 to door)
***Khana* rod length**	66" (1.67m)
Hole spacing	12" (30cm)
Holes per rod	6
Total wall rods (including rods to be cut to make ends)	56 (42 full rods +14 for ends)
End pieces (angled)*	5 down (2), 3 down (2), 6 up (2), 4 up (2), 2 up (2)
End pieces (square)**	5 down (2), 4 down (1), 3 down (1), 2 down (1), 5 up (2), 4 up (1), 3 up (1), 2 up (1)

Sixteen foot yurt

Yurt diameter	16' (4.9m)
Wall height	5' (1.5m) (effective wall height 6' [1.83m])
Roof height	9' (2.74m)
Number of *khana*	3
Door height	6' (1.83m)
Door width (internal)	34" (86cm)
***Tono* diameter**	41" (1.05m)
***Tono* holes** (number and angle)	38 30º
***Uni* length**	96" (2.44m)
Bend (angle and distance from bottom)	15" (38cm) 35º
Number of *uni*	38 (35 to *khana*, 3 to door)
***Khana* rod length**	78" (1.98m)
Hole spacing	12" (30cm)
Holes per rod	7
Total wall rods (including rods to be cut to make ends)	78 (56 full rods + 22 for ends)
End pieces (angled)*	7 down (2), 5 down (2), 3 down (2), 7 up (2), 5 up (2), 3 up (2).
End pieces (square)**	6 down (4), 5down (2), 4 down (2), 3 down (2), 2 down (2), 6 up (4), 5 up (2), 4 up (2), 3 up (2), 2 up (2).

CHAPTER 12

The weekend yurt

This chapter gives simple step-by-step instructions for the construction of a nine foot yurt. This proven design can, and has been built by absolute beginners. A full set of instructions is given, which can be used on its own, so there will be some repetition of the basic skills.

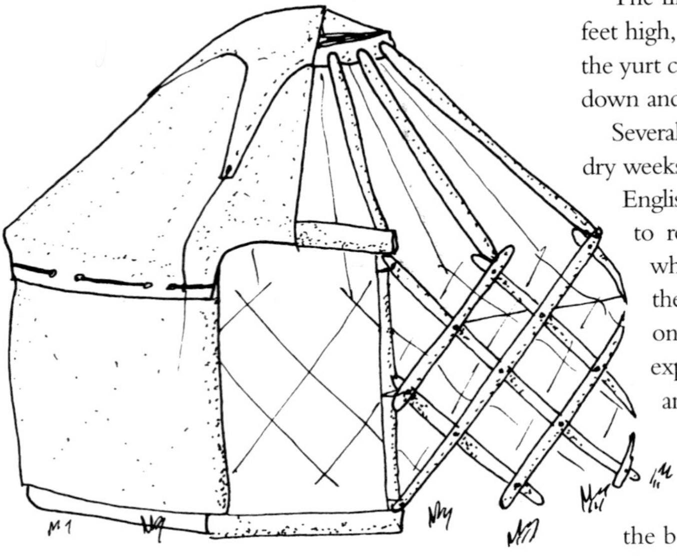

Fig. 72: The dissected weekend yurt

The weekend *ger*

This is a simple design for a small, but extremely useful and robust yurt. It can be built by anyone who can use the most simple woodworking tools. It has been built by absolute beginners in less than three days, including the time spent selecting and cutting the poles. The cover will take another two or three days to complete.

The finished yurt will be nine feet wide, six feet high, with three-foot-six walls. Once made the yurt can be erected in 30 minutes, and taken down and packed in half this time (*fig 72*).

Several families have spent comfortable and dry weeks in these *gers* over cold, wet and windy English summers. A number have been sold to replace brand new conventional tents which had been flooded or blown away; the *gers* suffered no such fate. I have left one standing in my garden all winter exposed to gale force winds, continuous, and torrential rain. The yurt has stood with no attention whatsoever, and the contents have remained dry.

The entire *ger* can be carried in the boot of a Mini Metro. Two people can comfortably carry it a considerable distance, to be away from the road, or to take it on public transport. It forms a spacious home for two people and has ample room for two adults and three children, while still leaving room for storage and cooking.

Materials

For the frame

For this example I have suggested willow, which is simple to work with and fairly easy to find; try one of the many farmers growing willow as a biomass fuel. Coppiced hazel, ash, sweet chestnut or any other straight, roundwood poles can be used.

Straight willow rods exactly 54" (1.37m) long, ¾-1" (19-25mm) dia	**40**
Straight willow rods exactly 30" (76cm) long, ¾-1" (19-25mm) dia	**2**
Straight willow rods exactly 28" (71cm) long, ¾-1" (19-25mm) dia	**2**
Straight willow rods exactly 60" (1.52m) long, ¾-1½" (19-38mm) dia	**20**
Straight willow rods exactly 48" (1.22m) long, 1-1½" (25-38mm) dia	**2**
Length of round-wood exactly 32" (81.3cm)long, 2-3" (50-75mm) dia	**2**
5' (1.52m) length of 9"x1¼" (23x32mm) planed timber	
3' (1m) length of 3"x1" (75x25mm) planed timber	
100' (30m) of Cardoc J (4mm) nylon cord (or similar)	
35' (11m) of strong rope	
Wood glue	
Screws 6 x1"	**20**

For the cover

- 12oz fire, water and rot-proofed cotton canvas (or similar) (30m)
- Plastic-coated fabric (a piece 26' [7.92m] long and 10" [25cm] wide)
- ⅜" (10mm) brass grommets (eyelets) (50)
- Strong polyester thread (400m)

Tools

For the frame

- Tape measure
- Loppers or pruning-saw
- Curved knife
- Electric drill
- ³⁄₁₆ inch (4.5mm) drill bit
- ⅜ inch (10mm) drill bit
- Cigarette lighter
- Jig-saw (or coping saw)
- Hand saw
- Drill brace
- ⅞ inch (22mm) auger drill bit
- Screwdriver
- Set square
- Sliding bevel
- G-clamps (at least 4)
- Surform tool or electric sander/planer

For the cover

- Sewing machine
- Scissors
- Protractor
- Pins

Fig. 73: Hole spacing for the *khana* rods

Preparing the wood

Cut wood (2 hours)
If you are using coppice wood: willow, hazel or sweet chestnut, are all ideal. Cut the wood during the winter months if possible, this reduces harm to the trees and to woodland wildlife. If you must cut during the summer just take a few shoots from each stool (tree). Select straight poles and cut them near the base. To reduce the risk of fungal infection to the tree, make the cut as clean as possible and angled to allow water to run off.

Cut willow exactly to length (60 minutes)
Cut the rods exactly to the required length. For the wall rods measure around any slight curves. For curved or bent roof rods measure a straight line between the two ends (*fig 27*).

Strip the willow (90 minutes)
Stripping the bark gives an attractive, light finish; for a more rustic appearance leave the bark on. Always remove any sharp knots or twigs, which might damage the cover. If willow is freshly cut the bark can easily be pulled off by hand and any knots removed with a sharp knife. Dry willow or hazel can be stripped using a curved knife.

The walls *khana*

Drill wall rods (60 minutes)
Most of the rods will taper slightly, giving a distinct thick and thin end. For maximum strength you will need an equal number of rods with the thick end, and thin end at the top. Any slightly curved poles should be drilled in the same plane as the bend (*fig 28*).

Start at the top end; i.e. the thick end for 18 rods and the thin end for the other 18. Drill the first 4.5mm hole 2 inches (50mm) from the top, followed by another four holes, 12 inches (30cm) apart (*fig 73*).

Drill the four 28 inch (71cm) and 30 inch (76cm) rods at 2 inches (50mm), 14 inches (35.6cm) and 26 inches (66cm) from one end.

Smooth ends of wall and roof poles (30 minutes)
Use a sharp knife or a surform tool to round off both ends of each wall rod (*fig 74*).

Fig. 74: The finished rod end

Also smooth the thick end of each roof pole.

Tie the wall *khana* (3 hours)

Take 36 wall rods and tie them together to form the *khana*. The rods should, traditionally, rise from the left at the base, and to the right at the top. Start with two tops together; one thin and one thick. Keep alternating thick and thin tops as you go. Any curved poles should point inwards (towards the centre of the yurt) at the ends, with the middle bowing outwards.

To ease the pushing of the string through the holes carefully heat about an inch (25mm) of the string and roll it in your fingers to form a sort of needle; beware of the obvious risk of burning your fingers. Pull the string and tie the knots as tight as possible. If you cannot pull the knots sufficiently tight – tie another knot by winding the free end of the string behind the first one. When you are happy with the knot, burn off the string using a cigarette lighter.

When the 36 rods are joined use four short lengths to fill in the gap at either end. All holes at each end of the *khana* should be tied using a piece of string with a loop in one end and about 12 inches (30cm) of free cord left after the knot at the other. These strings and loops will secure the door in place (*fig 75*).

To ensure that the *khana* is spread correctly when you put up the yurt. Open the *khana* so that each 'diamond' is exactly 16¼ inches (41cm) wide and tie a piece of cord between each of the second knots down. Pull the cord fairly tight and measure each 'diamond' as you go.

The crown *tono*

The crown is made by laminating eight sections together, to form a strong wheel to support the tops of the roof poles. Ideally use English oak or beech; if these are not available knot-free pine will suffice.

Preparing the crown sections (90 minutes)

Make a template using card or hardboard. Draw a circle 18 inches (45cm) in diameter. Draw another circle 12½ inches (31cm) in diameter, inside the first. Draw a cross in the middle of the circles to divide them exactly into four. Carefully cut out one of the quarters, hold the cut quarter over the remaining three to check that it is exactly the same size.

Use the hardboard template to mark out eight sections, use a sharp pencil or ball point

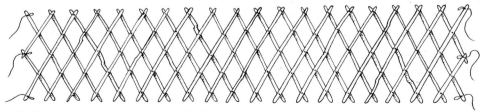

Fig. 75: The complete *khana* for a nine foot weekend yurt

pen and take care to mark as accurately as possible without moving the template.

Cut around the curved outlines of the sections using a jig-saw. Use a hand saw for more accurate cutting of the straight edges.

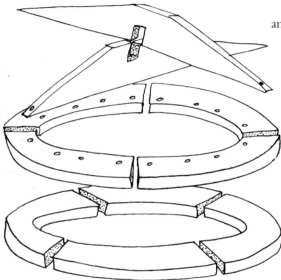

Fig. 76: An exploded view of the *tono*

Assembling the crown sections (60 minutes)

Lay four crown sections on the bench, to form the best possible circle. Lay another four sections on top of these, ensuring that the joints on the top layer occur midway between the joints on the bottom. These sections will be screwed and glued together. Mark both sides of

each joint so that they can be put back in the same order. Mark the desired position for eight screw holes; screws must be near the inside of the circle so that they will not interfere with later drilling of the crown. Drill the 4mm screw-holes and countersink with a 10mm bit.

Lay the prepared sections out as described and apply PVA wood-glue to the mating surfaces of two of the upper sections. Screw these exactly into place and clamp the sections together using at least four G-clamps. Allow the glue to set. Use glue, screws and clamps, as described, to join the remaining four sections and complete the circle.

Finishing the inner and outer crown surfaces (60 minutes)

Use a surform tool, electric sander, or planer to remove waste timber and give a smooth, even inner and outer rim to the crown.

Drilling the crown (60 minutes)

Measure the outside circumference of the crown and divide this figure by 20. Mark 20 equally spaced points around the outer edge of the crown. Avoid the joints between sections; if necessary adjust the spacing of the holes.

Use a shaving horse or similar bench to support the crown, position the crown at an angle of 39° from the vertical. Use a piece of waste wood nailed or clamped to the bench to support the crown in position (*fig 77*).

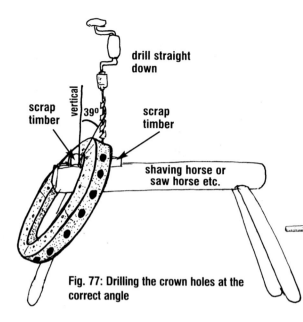

Fig. 77: Drilling the crown holes at the correct angle

Drill the 20 holes using a brace and 22mm bit. Drill all holes to the same depth. Do not drill so deep that the bit breaks through the top of the crown

Making the raised crown centre (60 minutes)

Take two 18 inch (45cm) lengths of planed 3x1 inch (75x25mm) timber. Mark the centre of one of the edges on each length, and then mark a point 2 inches (50mm) either side of the middle. Draw lines from each of the 2 inch marks to the bottom corner on each side. Cut along these lines (*fig 76*). Measure the exact thickness of the timber and cut a slot in the centre of one piece 1½ inches (38mm) deep in the top. Cut an equivalent slot in the bottom of the other. These pieces can now be assembled and screwed and glued to the crown.

The roof
Drill roof poles *uni* (30 minutes)

Drill 4.5mm holes at 1 inch (25mm) and 2 inches (50mm) from the thick end of 18 of the rods. If any rods are slightly curved drill at 90° to the plane of the curve. Leave two rods un-drilled (*fig 78*).

Drill roof poles at 90° to plane of curve

Fig. 78: Holes in the roof pole to take the securing loop

Tie the roof securing loops (30 minutes)

Find a piece of scrap willow of the same diameter as a typical wall pole top. Tie a string loop, which passes through the two holes in each of the 18 drilled roof poles. Use your piece of scrap willow as a gauge to ensure the correct size of loop (*fig 79*).

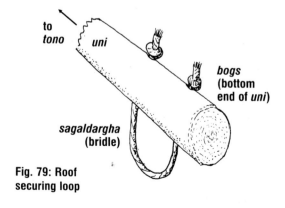

Fig. 79: Roof securing loop

Shape the top end of the roof poles (30 minutes)

Drill a ⅞ inch (22mm) hole in a scrap piece of timber, use this as a gauge. Use a sharp knife to shape the top 3 inches of each roof pole so that it fits loosely into the gauge hole.

The door
Making the door frame (30 minutes)

Drill two 1 inch (25mm) holes 28 inches (71cm) apart in each of the 32 inch (81cm) lengths of 2-3 inch (50-75mm) round-wood. Shave the ends of the two 48 inch (1.22m) rods to fit tightly into these holes. Assemble the door frame. Lay the door on the ground and drill two further holes,

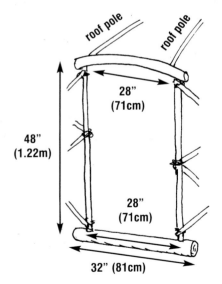

Fig. 80: Door frame

angled slightly upwards, to take the roof poles (*fig 80*).

Your yurt frame is now finished, and ready to assemble.

Assembling the frame

Putting up your yurt (30 minutes)

1. Unfold the wall section and place it upright in an approximate circle.
2. Tie the two ends to the door frame.
3. Adjust the position of the walls until they are perfectly circular. Use two poles held end-to-end to check that the diameter is exactly the same at several points.
4. Tie a strong rope around the top of the walls. **This step is very important**; to fit the roof without this band around the yurt will cause serious damage.
5. Fit the string loop of each roof pole over the top of an inner wall pole so that the end sits in the V.
6. Ask a friend to hold the crown above their head in the centre of the yurt. Insert the top ends of the roof poles into the holes in the crown.
7. Pull the crown hard down to ensure that it is level and that all the roof poles are securely seated.
8. Fit the cover.

■ **Total time: 17½ hours**

The cover *twrga*

The traditional covering for the yurt is felt, made by beating and rolling wet sheep fleece. It takes the wool of 100 sheep to cover the typical Mongolian *ger*. A more practical covering can be made using cotton canvas. We use 12oz canvas which has been fire, water and rot-proofed. You will need 30m of canvas. A waterproof PVC skirt protects the bottom of the wall poles and canvas. The canvas can be sewn on most domestic sewing machines. The old black Singer hand machines are ideal. You can find one at any car boot sale or auction for about £10. Use strong polyester thread for all sewing. It will take two or three days to make the cover.

The wall

Take a 29 foot 6 inch (9m) length of canvas and make a 3 inch (75mm) hem at each end. Take a length of PVC-coated fabric 26 feet (7.9m) long and 10 inches (25cm) wide and sew it to the bottom of the canvas leaving 18 inches (45cm) free at each end. Overlap the two pieces by one inch and sew with a double seam. Cut holes and

fit grommets at the top, bottom and middle of each end hem. Tie two foot (60cm) lengths of cord through each grommet. Cut holes and fit grommets close to the top of the wall at 33½ inches (85cm) intervals, with the first one 36 inches (91cm) from one end. Tie a 6 inch (15cm) length of cord into a loop through each of these grommets (*fig 81*).

The tension band

Take a piece of canvas 59 inches (150cm) long and cut it lengthways into six equal pieces. Sew these pieces together, end-to-end. Fold each end over to form a blunt point and sew into place. Sew a hem along each side of the band. Fit a grommet and attach a 3 foot (1m) length of rope to each end (*fig 82*).

Fig. 82: The tension band

Roof cover
Step one:

Take two lengths of canvas: one 13 feet 6 inches (4.12m) and the other 14 feet (4.27m)

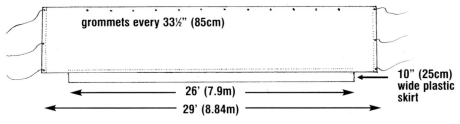

grommets every 33½" (85cm)

10" (25cm) wide plastic skirt

26' (7.9m)

29' (8.84m)

Fig. 81: The complete wall cover

long. Sew the two together with a one-inch overlap and a double seam: sew all sheets of canvas in this way. Prepare a length of canvas, square at one end, and cut at 45° at the other. The length at the shorter edge should be 78 inches (1.88m). Cut another piece exactly the same. Sew these two pieces of canvas to the 14 foot (4.26m) length as shown (*fig 83*).

Step two
Lay the canvas on the floor, or with the overlapping angled ends resting on a table. Adjust the angle between the outer edges of

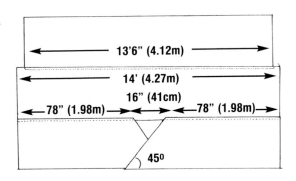

Fig. 83: The cover blank: stage one

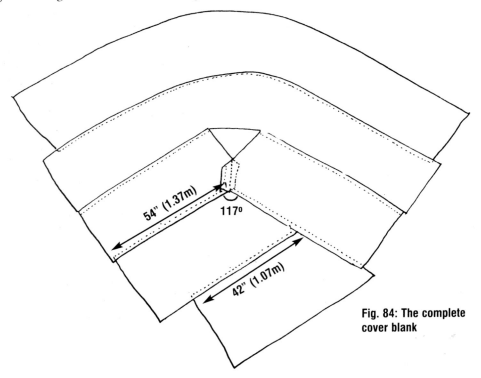

Fig. 84: The complete cover blank

the two angled sheets to exactly 117°, ensure that the overlapping parts are lying flat on the table and that the gap between the adjacent sheets forms an approximate equilateral triangle. Carefully pin the sheets together in a straight line between the tip of the triangle and the 117° angle.

Sew along the line of pins. Cut the spare ends away, parallel to this seam, leaving a good two inches (50mm) of canvas each side. Fold the cut edges under and sew into place.

Now cut two pieces, square at one end, with a 117° angle at the other; one piece should be 54 inches (1.37m) and the other 42 inches (1.07m) long, measured at the shorter edge. Sew these sheets into place (fig 84).

Fitting the cover

For the next stage you will need to put up your yurt frame to fit the cover. If working outside choose a dry day with no wind. Put up the yurt frame and place the roof cover over it. The edge of the 13 foot 6 inch (4.12m) sheet should be above the door, with the angled sheets to the back. Make sure it is the right way up: the top sheets should overlap the lower ones to allow water run-off. Position the central triangular hole over the crown and adjust the cover so that the ends hang down as far as possible at the back and sides and the front sheet overlaps the door top by 3-4 inches (75-100mm).

Cut around the overhanging ends parallel with the ground and about ten inches (25cm) below the top of the wall. Use two of the triangular pieces you have cut off to fill the gaps next to the door: pin them in position (fig 85).

Make about eight tucks in the overhanging cover to make this part parallel with the walls; do not make the cover too tight fitting as it will shrink slightly when it gets wet. Pin these tucks and mark the top end with a pencil. Make two further tucks at the top corners of the door. You may need to do some fine adjustments with the scissors to make the lower edge straight again.

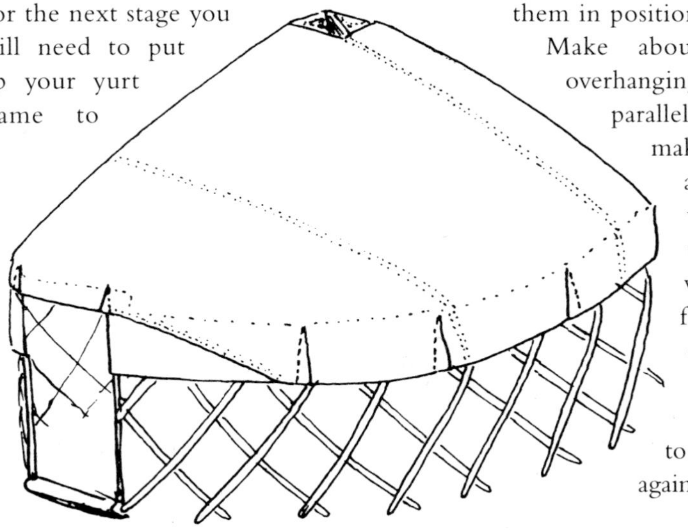

Fig. 85: Final fitting of the roof cover

Mark a circle corresponding to the crown opening, and mark the bottom edge in several places so that you can identify the inside later.

Take the cover off and return to the sewing machine. Sew up all of the tucks around the edge, and above the door.

Sew a two-inch (50mm) hem all around the bottom edge and next to the door. Make sure the hem is on the inside.

Cut around the inside of the central circle, about half an inch (12mm) inside the line, fold this edge over and sew around, following the line. If you like, sew webbing tape around this hole for a neater edge.

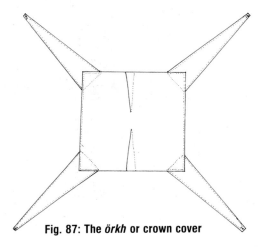

Fig. 87: The _örkh_ or crown cover

Make small holes and fit grommets in pairs six inches (15cm) apart every two feet around the bottom hem (_fig 86_).

The crown cover _örkh_

Cut out a 37 inch (98cm) length of canvas and sew a small hem along the two cut ends. Lay this piece over the crown and make a tuck either side so that it is a snug fit. Sew up these tucks and then sew a triangle of canvas to each corner. Put a grommet near the end of each triangle and attach about 8 feet (2.5m) of strong cord (_fig 87_).

The door

Cut a piece of canvas 54 inches (1.37m) long and make a 2½ inch (60mm) hem at

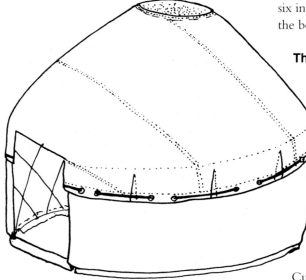

Fig. 86: The fitted cover

The weekend yurt

either end. Put three metal hooks in the door top, and three corresponding grommets in the door. If required, you can weight the bottom of the door by sliding a piece of wood inside the hem.

Fitting the cover

1. Put up the frame
2. Tie the end of the tension band inside the door and pull it around the top of the walls, where the roof poles join. Tie the other end inside the door.
3. Tie one end of the wall inside of the door and hang the string loops over alternate *khana* tops. Tie the other end inside the door.
4. Place the roof cover in place. Tie a rope inside the door and pass it through the grommets in the bottom hem of the cover. Tie the other end inside the door.
5. Fit the door.
6. Fit the crown cover, tie it in place.
7. If you are likely to experience high winds peg the yurt down using four guy ropes attached to the roof cover rope.
8. Live in your yurt and have lots of fun.

Happy yurting!

Sources of materials

Here are a few useful names, telephone numbers and ideas for the supply of materials for your yurt:

Canvas

- **Tony Beal Ltd. (Glasgow)**
  Tel: 0141 773 2166

- **Mitco (Romford)**
  Tel: 020 8590 6070

- **Tarpaulin Services (Exeter)**
  Tel: 01392 432228

- **Lows (Dundee)**
  Tel: 01382 229251

Sawn green oak or ash battens

Local timber merchants often only sell softwoods or imported timber. For locally grown timber try woodland estates, the Forestry Commission, your local community forest, or specialist timber suppliers.

Hazel poles

Try your local Wildlife Trust or woodland estate manager.

Willow poles

Try one of the many farmers growing willow as a biomass fuel.

String, glue, varnish, grommets etc.

Any local hardware shop.

Glossary

(M)=Mongolian (T)= Turkic

Airag (M): Fermented mare's milk
Arag (M): Wicker basket for collecting fuel
Äq (T): Bentwood yurt
Bagana (M): Upright posts to support *tono*
Boorts (M): Dried meat
Bosgogh (M): Bottom of door frame
Buheg (M): Tipi-like tent used by Tsaatan people
Burees (M): Felt collar around crown opening
Busluur (M:) Tension bands on Mongol *ger*
Buuz (M): Meat dumplings
Çevlic (T): Bentwood roof wheel
Chagata (M): Rope to hold *tono* down in strong wind
Coppice: Method of tree cutting to produce straight poles
Crown: Wheel at centre of yurt roof
Deever (M): Felt roof cover
Del (M): Traditional Mongol coat
Düynük (T): Bentwood roof wheel
Ers (M): Feet: Bottom ends of *khana* poles
Esgi (M): Felt
Felt: Fabric made by beating and rolling wool
Foot: Bottom of *khana* poles (See Ers)
Ger (M): Mongolian yurt
Gerlug (M): *Ger* permanently mounted on a cart
Ger uhn Booreess (M): Decorative cotton *ger* cover

Hâne (T): Two-tiered yurt
Head: Top of *khana* poles
Hirgâ (T): Two-tiered yurt
Khalga (M): Door
Khana (M): Trellis wall panel
Khar mod (M): Single *khana* rod
Khoimor (M): Sacred part at back of *ger*
Khoohoor (M): *Airag* bag
Oba (T): Bentwood yurt
Örgöö (M): Very large *ger*
Örkh (M): Crown cover
Ovoo (M): Sacred cairn
Öy (T): Bentwood yurt
Sagaldarga (M): Loop attaching *uni* to *khana*
Tension band: Cloth band to prevent roof pushing walls outwards
Tension rope: Rope to prevent roof pushing walls outwards
Terim (T): Trellis wall panel
Tolgoi (M): Head: Top of *khana* rods
Tono (M): Crown, roof wheel
Totgo (M): Lintel: top of door frame
Tsamkhraa (M): Spoke in centre of *tono*
Tulga (M): Traditional iron open brazier
Twrga (M): Felt *ger* cover
Üdeer (M): Knotted leather joining *khana* rods
Uni (M): Roof pole
Urts (M): Tipi used by Tsaatan people (see *Buheg*)
Uvoljo (M): Winter camping ground
Zuukh (M): Metal stove

Bibliography

Andrews, Peter Alford, 1997. *Nomad tent Types of the Middle East: Part 1: Framed Tents* (two volumes). Dr Ludwig Reichert. Wiesbaden.

Allen, Benedict, 1998. *Edge of Blue Heaven: A journey through Mongolia.* BBC, London.

Anon. 1973. *Shelter.* Shelter Publications, Inc Calif.

Becker, Jasper, 1992. *The Lost Country: Mongolia Revealed.* Hodder and Stoughton, London.

Blue Evening Star, 1995. *Tipis and* Yurts: *Authentic designs for circular shelters.* Lark Books, Asheville, North Carolina, USA.

Bruun, Ole and Ole Odgaard (ed.) 1996. *Mongolia in Transition: Old Patterns, New Challenges.* Curzon, Richmond, Surrey.

Charmichael, Peter. 1991. *Nomads.* Collins and Brown, London.

Cleaves, Francis Woodman (translator). 1982. *The Secret History of the Mongols.* Harvard University Press.

Curtin, Jeremiah. 1908. *The Mongols: A History.* Combined Books, Pennsylvania.

Damdinsurengyn Altangerel. 1988. *How did the Great Bear originate?: Folktales from Mongolia.* State Publishing House, Ulaan Baatar.

Dineley, Mark. 1935. *The Turkomans of Persia.* The Geographical Magazine, Vol.1, No. 2, June 1935, pp. 151-162.

Dojoogyn Tsedev (ed.), 1989. *Modern Mongolian Poetry.* State Publishing House, Ullan Baatar.

Douglas, William O. 1962. *Journey to Outer Mongolia.* National Geographic. Vol. 121, No.3, March 1962. pp 289-345.

Faegre, Torvald. 1979. *Tents: Architecture of the Nomads.* John Murray, London.

Fairlie, Simon. 1996. *Low-impact Development.* Jon Carpenter, Oxfordshire.

Federation of City Farms and Community Gardens 2001. *The Yurt Education Pack: Linking the cultural, social and environmental aspects of the yurt.* Activities and Discussion Topics for 5 to 13-year-olds,

Fine Woodworking (ed), 1985. *Bending Wood.* The Taunton Press, Newtown, CT. Greenway, Paul. Story, Robert. Latiffe, Gabriel.

Bibliography

1997. *Mongolia: Travel Survival Kit* (2nd Ed.). Lonely Planet. Victoria, Australia.

Herodotus, c480–425BC, 1996. *Histories*. Trans: George Rawlinson. Wordsworth Classics.

Huc, Evarist-Regis. Joseph Gabet, William Hazlitt. 1846. *Travels in Tartary, Thibet, and China*. Asian Education Services.

Jagchid, Sechin and Paul Hyer. 1979. *Mongolia's Culture and Society*. Westview Press. Boulder, Colarado.

King, P. R. 1998. *Build your own Yurt: A complete guide to making a Mongolian ger* (third Ed.) P. R. King, Clevedon.

King, P.R. 1999. *The Weekend Yurt: Make a Mongolian ger in two weekends, simple step-by-step instructions*. P. R. King, Clevedon.

King, P.R. 1999. *Ger: the Mongolian Yurt*. Skyviews. Issue 14. pp13–15.

Marco Polo (1254-1329), 1997. *The Travels*. Translated by William Marsden (1818). Wordsworth Classics, Ware, Hertfordshire.

Marshall, Robert. 1993. *Storm From The East: From Ghengis Khan to Kublai Khan*. Penguin/BBC Books. Michaud, Roland and Sabrina. 1985. *Caravans to Tartary*. Thames and Hudson, London.

Murray, Edward, 1936. *With the Nomads of Central Asia*. National Geographic. Vol.69. No.1, January 1936. pp 1–57.

Place, Steve, 1997. *How to build a Yurt*. Centre For Alternative Technology Factsheet. CAT, Machynlleth.

Sinclair, Kevin. 1987. *The Forgotten Tribes of China*. Merehurst Press, London

Sjöberg, Gunilla Paetau, 1996. *Felt: New directions for an ancient craft*. Interweave Press Inc, Colorado.

Structure Constructor, 1997. *How to build your low-impact dwelling*. Structure Constructor, Yorkshire.

Trippett, Frank, 1978. *The first horsemen*. (*The Emergence of Man series*) Time-Life Books.

Tseltum N. 1988. *Mongolian Architecture*. State Publishing House, Ulaan Bataar.

Twitchett, D. and J.K. Fairbank, 1991. *The Cambridge history of China (vol. 15)*. Cambridge University Press.

Yunden Ya., Zorig G., Erdene Ch. 1991. *This is Mongolia. Ulaan Baatar.*

Yurt makers

UK
Woodland Yurts
80 Coleridge Vale Road South
Clevedon, North Somerset BS21 6PG
Tel: 01275 879705
www.woodlandyurts.com

Turkoman Gers
Hullasey Barn, Tarlton, Cirencester
Gloucestershire GL7 6PA

Handmade Hardwood Yurts
Llan Farmhouse, Hirnant, Penybontfawr
near Oswestry, Powys SY10 0HP

USA
Nesting Bird Yurt Company
6999 Silver Springs Lane, NE Poulsbo, WA
98370

Pacific Yurts
77456 Highway 99, South Cottage Grove
Oregon 97424

Borealis Yurts
P.O. Box 985, Gray, ME 0439

Mongolia
The Monglian Artisans Aid Foundation
Ulaan Bataar-28, P.O. Box-329, Mongolia

ORD Co. Ltd.
Ulaan Bataar-23, P.O. Box-663, Mongolia

Woodland Yurts

Quality hand made Mongolian *gers*.
Bentwood and lightweight yurts.

●

All of our yurts are skilfully hand-crafted by experts. Frames
are made from locally-grown English hardwoods. Covers
are of heavy-duty treated cotton. Built to withstand the worst
of weather, or to make the most of the best summer days.

●

Prices from under £600 for a complete yurt.

●

Woodland Yurts
80 Coleridge Vale Road South
Clevedon, Somerset BS21 6PG, UK

☎ 01275 879705
www.woodlandyurts.com

eco-logic books

eco-logic books is a small, ethically-run company specialising in publishing and distributing books and other materials that promote practical solutions to environmental problems.

Those books that are still in print and mentioned in the further reading list plus many others are available from our website. Other topics covered include:

Peak Oil and Transition Thinking and Strategies
Gardening and Composting
Permaculture
Self Reliance
Food and related issues
Keeping Hens and other Domestic Animals
Smallholding and Farming
Sustainable Forestry, Woodland Crafts, and Wildlife
Orchards and Fruit Growing
Community
Building and Construction
Alternative Energy
Urban Issues and Transport
Money and the Economy
Trade Skills
Sustainabilty and Radical Thinking
Managing for Change

Download a **FREE** mail order catalogue from our website or send an s.a.e. to the address below:
eco-logic books
Mulberry House, 19 Maple Grove, Bath BA2 3AF
Telephone: 01225 484472   Fax: 0781 522 7054

www.eco-logicbooks.com